Schoolyard Mosaics

Designing Gardens and Habitats

National Gardening Association's

www.KidsGardening.org
www.GardeningWithKids.org

Writers: Eve Pranis, Amy Gifford
Illustrations: Suzanne Legault
Layout and production: Alison Watt

This book would not have been possible without inspiration and support from:

Pam Allan, Missouri City, TX
Linda Bartula, Missouri City, TX
Joanne Bauer, Southampton, PA
Irene Canaris, Westminster, VT
Phyllis Davidson, Charlottesville, VA
Mark Davis, Warren, PA
Joan Dungey, Yellow Springs, OH
Roger Earles, Santa Barbara, CA
Ann English, Athens, GA
Shirley Farrell, Leeds, AL
Diane Fuleihan, Westminster, VT
Rhonda Hancock, Phoenix, AZ
Ron Helstern, Hyrum, UT
Pam Irving, Bartlett, TN
Teddy Johnson, Athens, GA
Rosemary Johnston, Brook Park, OH
Rory Klick, Chicago Botanic Garden

Denise Krane, Brook Park, OH
Sue Luchs, Nashville, TN
Tina Margason, San Jose, CA
Ann Marischen, Chicago, IL
Julia Melloni, Burlington, VT
Vernon Mullens, San Antonio, TX
Tracy Penner, Vancouver, BC, Canada
Illene Pevec, Vancouver, BC, Canada
Karen Redel, Orlando, FL
Cynthia Ribish, Elm Grove, WI
Jean Sasabuchi, Vacaville, CA
Nancy Sklavos-Gillett, Mt. Olive, NJ
Kati Towle, Alexandria, VA
Kim Lowman Vollmer, Clinton, WI
Mark Warford, Schenectady, NY
Laurie Wedewer, Orlando, FL

First printing, 2003
Second printing, 2009
Library of Congress Control Number: 2002116896
ISBN-10: 0-915873-44-3
ISBN-13: 978-0-915873-44-9

Contents

Building a Vision

Many schoolyards are simple in design, with lawns for running and playgrounds for climbing. Some are seas of asphalt or construction dump sites. We hope you are reading this book because you are among the growing rank of teachers who believe the schoolyard can be much, much more: a vibrant outdoor classroom where kids are engaged in self-directed explorations of the natural world. But where to begin? The key to creating a one-of-a-kind schoolyard is to put some time and energy into building a vision that meets the needs of your classroom, school, and community.

Finding Inspiration

When it comes to transforming a schoolyard, the possibilities are endless. Before getting into grids and plans, tools and beds, take some time to dream and let your imaginations run wild. The school profile Imagining Special Places (right) describes one way to grease the wheels.

Another approach is to devote some time to researching other projects and making connections with people who are garden savvy. You will, no doubt, unearth a cornucopia of possibilities. Teachers at Brookpark Memorial School (page 27) spent two years visiting school gardens before transforming an abandoned courtyard into a learning laboratory. Consider these other strategies for finding inspiration:

- Visit school garden Web sites or other garden-related Web pages.
- Take a class or committee field trip to a local botanic garden or series of neighborhood gardens. (You can also take "virtual" field trips online through some botanic gardens!)
- After visiting other sites, have students draw or write about features that captured their imaginations.
- Invite local experts, including landscape architects, county Cooperative Extension agents, and Master Gardeners, to brainstorm with your group. You can do the same with teachers, parents, and other interested community members.

Considering Your Goals and Curriculum

It can be delightful to muse about your vision, but it's also important to consider *why* you're creating a schoolyard garden or habitat. This may affect your design. For example, if you want to provide habitat for wildlife, you'll need to make sure your design meets the food, water, and shelter requirements for the creatures you are trying to attract. Begin by considering the question, *What are our goals for creating a school garden?* Here are some possibilities:

- to beautify the school grounds and neighborhood
- to grow food for the school or community
- to increase hands-on science (or multidisciplinary) learning opportunities

Imagining Special Places

To prepare her students for carving out a garden site in the schoolyard, middle school teacher Joan Dungey in Yellow Springs, OH, invited them to reflect on and write about their favorite childhood places. Students next shared their stories with a partner, and each pair presented highlights to the rest of the class. "I found it interesting that nearly all of the students recalled some sort of peaceful natural spot where they had played or explored the world as youngsters," notes Joan. As students shared their images, classmates took notes and discussed similarities and patterns they noticed, then began to identify features they would like to see in their own outdoor learning center. "Because one of our goals was building community partnerships, we also considered who else might use the area and how we could meet their needs," says Joan. The garden design the students dreamed up included herb and flower gardens with benches for peaceful reflection and a switchgrass maze to challenge and delight students and the community. "Although the entire garden is a living laboratory for different studies, it's nice that it also reflects students' sense of special places," says Joan.

> *"If we want to prepare students to live in a democratic culture, they need to learn how to work with others to make decisions and solve problems that arise. What better place to practice than in a garden project?"*
>
> *— fourth grade teacher Sarah Elwood*

- to create a therapeutic environment
- to restore native plants
- to provide a springboard for improving student nutrition
- to teach responsibility and cooperation

You'll also want to consider how you can use the garden project to reach your curriculum goals. Gardens are well documented as meaningful contexts for student inquiry and for building an understanding of science concepts, but they can also help you add life and depth to a host of other curriculum areas. Beyond enriching the traditional subject areas, such as math and language arts, gardening projects provide fertile ground for addressing standards in personal development and social skills. By ensuring and demonstrating that your garden project truly integrates with the curriculum, you'll also increase your chances of garnering school funds to start or sustain it—which can be vital.

Cultivating Decision Makers: Students Take the Lead

"Since my school had adopted an approach to teaching and learning that encourages student choice and problem solving, we decided to apply that thinking to the garden project," says teacher Teddy Johnson from Chase Street Elementary School in Athens, GA. Teddy admits to having some doubts about her young charges' capacity to take on that level of responsibility, but took the risk to see what might unfold. "An important and very powerful aspect of our approach was to close every discussion and meeting by asking, *What do we need to know? What is our next step?*" says Teddy. "This seemed to provide a structure for the conversation that helped students move forward."

After a committee of students looked at the site and learned from parent/landscape architect Ann English about garden design concepts, students were inspired to try a butterfly-shaped butterfly garden. The question, *What do we need to know next?* prompted a discussion about the need to learn about butterfly life

Continued on page 6

Mapping the Curriculum

When planning your curriculum, look at the concepts, skills, and attitudes or dispositions that have been defined for your grade by local, state, or national standards. Which objectives might dovetail with garden-based experiences? Are there lessons you already teach in the classroom, about plant reproduction, for instance, that might be extended into or enhanced by a garden?

Think about how you could use your curriculum objectives to inform the design of the school garden. For instance, an ethnic or multicultural garden project can prompt students to dig into the cultures represented in the school and community, or those covered in the social studies curriculum. It might feature culturally relevant plants, appropriate planting techniques, and a visitors' guide detailing traditional plant uses, preparation, and folklore. A pollinator garden, on the other hand, is a great context for exploring core science concepts such as plant/animal interdependence, honing observation skills, and learning about environmental stewardship. In the end, remember that your teaching and learning goals will surely change over time and that you may have to adjust your growing plans accordingly.

Engaging Students as Planners and Decision Makers

Teachers across the country have discovered that when students are involved in all stages of the process, they are more invested in the project's success and inspired to care for and respect their schoolyard oases. By valuing students' opinions and encouraging them to make decisions, these educators have begun to cultivate motivated, confident, and collaborative learners. Teachers admit that relinquishing some control and inviting students into the decision-making process isn't necessarily easier or more efficient, but it is always rewarding.

How and how extensively you involve your students in planning and decision making will depend on your goals and comfort with letting go, and on their developmental abilities. You may decide to create a butterfly garden and simply offer students the opportunity to research and select plants, for instance. Or you might give students the reins throughout the entire planning and design process. The stories about Grandview U'uqinak'uuh Community School on page 31 and Chase Street Elementary School (left) highlight some exceptional ways to involve students.

Involving the School and Community

Thriving schoolyard garden projects often involve much, if not all, of the school community, so it's a good idea to get input early on from as many people as possible. This, of course, includes administrators, who can make or break a garden project. Many school gardeners will also tell you that custodians can be your greatest allies, since they're on the site year-round and know about water systems, traffic patterns, and so on. They will surely have cautions and creative ideas to add to your plan. Some or all of the teachers and classes may want to be involved in the design process, or simply take responsibility for specific planting beds or garden areas.

Among the most successful gardening programs are those in which educators and students have also reached out to cultivate partnerships in the broader community. (Lexington Creek Elementary School's program, featured on page 37, is one example.) These kinds of connections are important for obtaining materials and funds, but can be equally rewarding in nonmaterial ways. They help schools build bridges to the community and help local people better understand educational goals. By providing a focal point for positive interaction among all members of a neighborhood, a schoolyard oasis has the potential to foster collaboration and pride. But that's just the beginning of the benefits. Involving both the school and the neighborhood community in a schoolyard project:

- Promotes project sustainability because responsibilities don't fall entirely on the shoulders of one champion.
- Decreases the likelihood of vandalism because more people have a stake in the success of the program.
- Provides connections to potential volunteers and donors of labor, money, and products.
- Can encourage cross-generational mentoring and friendships among students, teachers, and a diversity of community members.
- Brings needed expertise and fresh ideas to the project.

A wise first step in getting others invested in your project is to involve them in the planning and design phase. Here are some suggestions for doing this.

Survey students, teachers, staff, and/or neighbors. Your students might design and conduct surveys to find out who currently uses different areas of the schoolyard, what they would like to see in the space, and what questions and concerns they have about the proposed project. The class might leave survey questions open-ended or provide a list of possible themes or features and ask participants to rank them based on their interests.

A hands-on approach to surveying students might include an activity called "hot-dotting." Provided with a map of the schoolyard, students can place hot (red or orange) sticker dots on areas of the schoolyard where they would like to spend time and cool (green or blue) dots on areas that are less enticing. This can provide a good jumping-off point for discussing which areas need to be improved and which are okay as is.

Have a curriculum meeting devoted to schoolyard design. Ask other teachers how they already use the schoolyard to address curriculum goals, and brainstorm design elements that might help them do so. Offer to share your thoughts on curriculum integration. As you consider specific design features, think about how to accommodate multiple classes. For instance, certain classes or grade levels might take responsibility for selected thematic beds or areas. Or cross-grade mentors might work together on specific projects.

Conduct a brainstorming session with potential supporters. This could include students, teachers, administrators, staff, parents, school board members, garden club members, college students in plant or agricultural sciences or educa-

Continued from page 5

cycles, the insects' tastebuds, garden design, and so on. "Ann and I tried to support students' efforts with resources and ideas when appropriate, but whenever possible let them take the lead," says Teddy. For instance, Ann helped students think about possible color schemes, but students had to brainstorm, discuss, and reach an agreement about the actual design. (The group agreed that the plants would be chosen to entice butterflies, but the concrete walkway down the center, which formed the butterfly's body, would be designed and painted to please the students!) "Because everyone was encouraged to share his or her opinion and work together to reach a compromise, both high- and low-end students were engaged in sharing and defending their ideas," notes Ann.

"It was very different working this way during the five-month planning process," says Teddy. "I had to be much more flexible to allow students time to puzzle out problems, listen to each other, and reach agreement before decisions were made," she explains. "Although the process was sometimes slow and tedious, the kids really did work through issues themselves. They learned that the responsibility for democracy can be challenging, but so can the gains," she adds.

No Site? Don't Fret!

If there's no room in the schoolyard for a garden, consider other site options: community gardens, city parks or lots, church properties, rooftops, nature centers, retirement centers, residential institutions, and housing developments. Once you locate a potential site, you'll need to get permission from the owner to use it. Ask about the future plans for the property, and try to set up a long-term arrangement. (If the owner is planning to construct a new building or parking lot, you are more likely to run into resistance from school administrators and will probably have to relocate your garden later on.) If these options are not feasible, consider gardening in containers.

4:00 p.m.   6-8 hours   10:00 a.m.

N

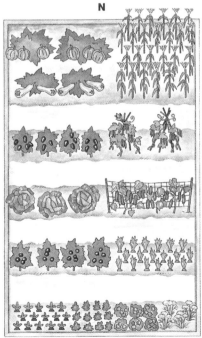

S

tion, farmers, Master Gardeners, staff from nurseries or businesses, landscape architects, and other interested community members. Students can spread the word by presenting the project idea at a faculty, school board, or PTO meeting and inviting people to join the brainstorming session. They might notify interested community members by hanging posters, sending out a newsletter, or announcing the upcoming session in the local newspaper or on radio or television.

Bringing the Vision to Life

Once you have crafted a vision for the schoolyard garden or habitat, it's time to get to work. The most important thing to remember is to start small. It is easy to get carried away by the excitement of a schoolyard transformation, but maintaining a huge garden area can be overwhelming for both you and the students. Setting short- and long-term goals will help you stage the process. Ask, *What is reasonable to accomplish this year given our funds, equipment, time, and people power? In five years?* Try to prioritize your goals and then write down what you hope to accomplish each year so you'll have targets to shoot for.

Assessing Your Site

Before putting your vision to paper and then into action, you'll want to find the best location and assess it in relation to your plan and the basic needs of plants. Here's where your young sleuths can begin to dig in. Use the questions in the box on page 8 to guide your thinking, and then plan accordingly.

Students might first identify basic plant needs—water, air, light, and nutrients—and assess how well different schoolyard locations meet them. Then they can ask what they can do to improve conditions. Here's some advice:

Water. Access to water is essential for gardening in most parts of the country, and the closer the water is to the garden, the better. Adding mulch (such as a layer of straw) around plants reduces water loss, but isn't practical for all plants. Bucket brigades can work in the early stages, but eventually the water needs a direct route to the garden via spigots or hoses. Oak Elementary School (page 29) has an automated irrigation system that turns on four times a week. It was installed free by a local business. Here are some other suggestions from school gardeners for garnering water:

- Get permission from neighbors to hook up a temporary line to their outdoor faucets.
- Ask permission from the local fire or water department to use a nearby fire hydrant.
- Tap into an existing underground municipal line running near the site. (Ask about installing a metered line.)
- Ask the fire department to fill up used storage tanks or 55-gallon steel drums periodically during the season. (Be sure these drums have not been used to store hazardous materials.)

Air. Plants need carbon dioxide to produce food through photosynthesis and oxygen for respiration. Excessive atmospheric pollution from major highways, industry smokestacks, and other sources can stunt many types of plants. If your only option is to garden in such a location, give your plants an extra advantage by providing rich, fertile soil and rinsing off the leaves every week. You should also stick with growing flowers, shrubs, and other ornamentals rather than food plants.

Light. Most flower, vegetable, and herb gardens need to be exposed to full sunlight for *at least* 6 hours a day. Students can check the potential garden site at different times during the day and year to see how much sun it receives. If it's winter, remember to factor in shade that will be cast by tree leaves. Use shady areas for gathering places or to plant shade-tolerant crops such as lettuce.

Soil Health and Nutrients. A nutrient-rich soil with good texture and plenty of organic matter will help your garden thrive. A site with 6 to 12 inches of topsoil is ideal, but often difficult to find. (A less accurate, but still reliable, indication of a good garden site is the presence of grass or a good crop of weeds.) If you do need to add topsoil, use this formula to calculate how many cubic yards you'll need:

Length of site (in feet) x width (in feet) x depth to be covered (in feet) = the cubic feet of topsoil needed. To convert to cubic yards, divide the number by 27.

By identifying your soil type and conducting some tests, you'll be better equipped to improve it. Here's how:

Identify the soil type. The texture of the soil, determined by its proportions of the minerals sand, silt, and clay, affects the water drainage and nutrient availability. Soils composed mainly of sand (the largest particles) can dry out too quickly and don't retain nutrients well, but do warm up early in the season. Dense clay soils (the smallest particles) can easily become water-saturated, which deprives roots of adequate oxygen. They are slow to warm in the spring, but are rich in nutrients. Silt, which has medium-sized particles, has a blend of these qualities. Loam is a soil type that has an intermediate texture and ideal nutrient and water holding ability.

Check your potential garden site to see if there are puddles after a hard rain, which indicate a high percentage of clay. If the soil is generally dry and drains quickly after a rain, it contains more sand. Whether you have dry sandy soil, silty soil, or wet clay soil, adding organic matter in its many forms, such as compost, will improve the soil structure and fertility. (The ideal proportion of organic matter in most soils is between 5 and 10 percent.) If you are just starting a garden and don't have any compost of your own, call the local Department of Public Works to find out if there is a municipal compost program in your town. You can also contact local farms, landscapers, and garden centers to see if they would be willing to donate compost.

Test soil nutrient and pH levels. Testing soil for pH (acidity) is a wise next step. Students can test the soil for pH and certain nutrients using a home test kit (available at garden centers and in the *Gardening with Kids* catalog), or they can contact your county Cooperative Extension office to find out where to send a sample for testing. Nutrients are most available to plants at pH levels between 6 and 7. If the pH of your soil is too low (< 7.0, acidic), you can add ground limestone to the soil to raise it. If the pH is too high (> 7.0, basic), you can add sulfur to lower it. The size of the garden and the results of the pH test determine the quantity you will need to spread to alter the pH.

Test for lead contamination, if necessary. Find out as much as possible about the history of your garden site before planting. You may want to have the soil tested for lead contamination if the site is in an urban area, is near houses or other structures that sported lead paint, was once used for dumping, is near a heavily traveled road, or was ever an orchard (fruit trees were once treated with a lead-based insecticide). Lead tests are not available in do-it-yourself kits. Call your local Cooperative Extension office, State Department of Agriculture, or Public Health Department to find out where to get soil tested. If your site is contaminated

Questions to Ask About Your Site

- Can the site be reached easily from classrooms?
- Is there access to a reliable water source?
- Is the site well drained?
- Does the site receive at least 6 hours of sunlight per day?
- How healthy is the soil? Do we have at least 6 inches of loose, rich soil? If not, what needs to be done to prepare or enhance it?
- Is the soil free of heavy metals such as lead?
- Is the site big enough for our draft design? Is there room for future growth?
- Is the site adversely exposed to pollutants from major highways, industry smokestacks, airports, or other sources?
- How long are we likely to be able to use this site?

Classrooms at Lower Southampton Elementary open out to the garden (story page 21).

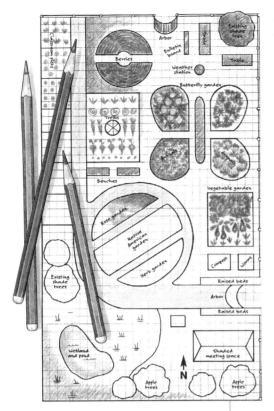

with lead, the simplest solution may be to find another site. Otherwise, you'll have to remove contaminated topsoil and replace it with clean soil.

Designing/Mapping the Site

The project highlights throughout the book feature some of the clever approaches teachers have used to involve students in mapping out gardens. Here, we offer some advice to get your creative juices flowing.

Your school garden might be small enough to require a simple planting map or it may entail many different types of features. If you are mapping a large site, you might want to consider a two-step process in which students first map out the "big" picture by identifying buildings, fences, trees, shrubs, play areas, and major pathways, and then create detailed plant maps of smaller areas, such as a rainbow garden.

In either case, students can measure the actual size of the proposed site and features and then use grid or graph paper and an appropriate scale to sketch the garden layout. (Make sure they add the four main compass directions.) You can give younger students the scale, 1 block = 1 foot or 10 feet, for instance. Challenge older students to figure out an appropriate scale.

Consider having each student or small group submit a "dream garden" design. Students might draw their visions or cut out images of garden plants from seed catalogs and paste them on paper. The class can then choose the best—and most practical—elements of each to incorporate into a final design. They might decide to circulate the formal design in the school and community to solicit comments and suggestions.

The concept of representing a three-dimensional garden space in one dimension can be difficult for students to grasp, especially young ones. Think about an intermediate step, like having students create a 3-D model using cardboard, natural materials, and/or a pliable medium, such as polymer clay.

Students can figure out planting schemes for different sections of the garden by consulting seed catalogs and packets, neighborhood gardeners, gardening books, and Internet sites. Such resources provide details on plant colors, heights, spacing needs, and so on. Imagine the possibilities for practicing teamwork and honing math and art skills as students puzzle out design details. *How much space does a bean tepee take up? How many square feet of wood chips will we need if we want them 4 inches deep on our paths? How can we split a circular bed into six even sections?*

If you have a large project, consider finding a local landscaper or similar professional who is willing to donate time. He or she can make sure you've considered all available options and potential problem areas, and help you move the design forward. Try to find someone who will engage students in the planning and design process.

Garden Features

In the garden and habitat designs that begin on page 14 you'll find a wide variety of components from handicapped-accessible pathways to permanent structures, such as gazebos. The companion stories highlight how school gardeners planned, funded, and implemented many of these features. Here are some tips on integrating some of the most common elements. (You'll find more in-depth information in many of the resources described on pages 52 to 55.) Consider where these might fit into your design and plan accordingly.

Garden beds. Your site might feature one or several group gardens, beds for individual students or classes, or both. (Sharing gardening responsibilities promotes teamwork, and individual plots can advance personal responsibility and pride.)

You can create garden beds in various shapes and sizes. If you keep the growing areas no wider than 3 or 4 feet, everyone involved in the program should be able to reach all plants. Although it is common to align rectangular beds evenly in rows, some school gardeners avoid doing so, explaining that it leaves little room for creative inspiration. Some try circular gardens, sliced, pie-fashion, by pathways. Others are inspired by the natural world. (Witness the butterfly-shaped garden on page 36.) You might arrange your planting beds in

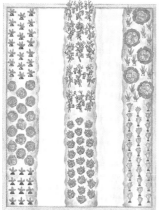

a circle or other geometric design around a central meeting area, or scatter beds of different sizes and shapes throughout the garden site.

Raised beds look nice, allow you to grow more in less space than flat beds do, and warm up and dry out faster in the spring. They also help plants, especially root crops, grow better because the soil is loose and fast-draining. (If you're gardening in the arid West or other places with dry soils and little rainfall, you may not want to use raised beds.) Finally, raised beds can be made accessible to wheelchair users. The simplest way to create a raised bed is to measure and stake each planting area, then loosen the soil with a spading fork and add soil, compost, or both until the bed is 8 to 12 inches high. Rake the surface smooth, shooting for a flat-topped bed. If you want to create permanent, well-defined raised beds, use rot-resistant wood, such as cedar or recycled plastic, bricks, rocks, or cement blocks. Don't use pressure-treated wood or railroad ties, because they may contain poisonous chemicals.

Paths. Paths reduce the risk that plants will get trampled, and they organize traffic flow. Make main pathways 4 feet wide to accommodate wheelchairs and wheelbarrows. Paths between small beds can be 30 inches wide. Keep paths distinct and weed-free. If steady foot traffic doesn't do the trick, you can cover paths with mulch, such as shredded bark or wood chips. (To help keep down weeds, lay down sheets of black and white newspaper, cardboard, or landscape fabric before mulching.) Alternatively, you can plant pathways with clover or mixed grass seed and have it mowed regularly. In permanent garden sites, you can use asphalt, bricks, pebbles, or crushed stone.

Gathering places. In a shady part of the garden, a picnic table, bench, or group of hay bales or logs provides an ideal place for cleaning and sorting vegetables, conducting outdoor lessons, doing arts and crafts, writing in journals, or just getting relief from the sun. You can provide protection from the elements by including a roof or awning. Some schoolyards sport natural amphitheaters created from grass mounds or benches placed in a semicircle. Others incorporate natural elements (log seating, for instance), cultural ones (Southwest "ramada" for shade), or artistic ones (mosaic tiles for sitting).

Living "rooms." Consider growing a hideaway or special place for reading, reflection, and writing. This could entail a group of bean tepees, a sunflower "house," or a living archway or tunnel with shrubs and vines.

- Bean tepees consist of five or more poles bound at the top and underplanted with pole beans.
- To grow a sunflower house, start by drawing a square or rectangle in the dirt the size you want the house to be. Plant seeds of tall sunflower varieties every 9 to 12 inches all around the perimeter of your square, leaving an

Planning Learning Landscapes: Students Lead the Way

The advent of the new millennium found Cynthia Ribish's Elm Grove, WI, sixth graders pondering how they could leave a legacy for future classes. A brainstorm session revealed students' interest in creating a less "prisonlike" schoolyard. "I seized the opportunity to have the class set goals and figure out how to meet them," says Cynthia.

First she challenged them to develop a guiding question. They settled on *How can we make our grounds more attractive and useful for the school and community?* To help structure the planning process, Cynthia created a worksheet with questions to guide students' thinking: *What are you trying to work on? From whom do you need help? What is the first step? When do you expect to achieve the goal?*

A group of students first toured the property, digital camera in hand, and identified which features they liked and which they wanted to change. Next, they surveyed other kids who would use and care about the space. A project wish list— a butterfly garden, observational walk, and so on—began to emerge.

The class divided the list into short- and long-term goals and prioritized them based on time and budget constraints and community feedback. This phase also involved research via Web sites, books, and visits to community gardens. Finally, the groups considered potential sources of support (e.g., Master

Continued on page 11

Continued from page 10

Gardeners) and created an action plan to guide their work. Student recorders published meeting notes on such topics as project progress and student responsibilities. "The students discovered that bringing their plans to life would proceed only as funding and support allowed," says Cynthia. With an eye toward persuading others to support their efforts, they created a PowerPoint presentation to describe their plans in images and text. By keeping the school district public relations person informed of their progress, they ensured that a broad audience would hear about the project.

"The students gained so much in their ability to set goals and determine how to reach them," says Cynthia. In fact, her kids use a graphic organizer routinely to provide evidence that they are achieving their goals, and if they are not, to identify what they need to do differently. "As important, their confidence soared along with their ability to recognize and respect their peers' skills and talents."

opening wide enough for a door on one of the sides. As the sunflowers grow, stake them if necessary. Plant morning glories or sweet peas around the base of each sunflower, and they will grow up the stems, eventually forming a roof over the top. (You can also substitute corn for sunflowers or intermingle the two.)

- Students can create a living tunnel by inserting 8-foot poles every 3 feet along both sides of a path. Next, lash horizontal poles at 2-, 4-, and 6-foot heights and then plant and train vines, such as clematis or morning glory, along the corridor.

You can create rustic arches, walls, and freeform sculptures from willow or other bendable twigs. Bury one or both ends of vertical sticks in the ground, then simply weave twigs (and/or grapevines) between them, overlapping as new ones are added.

Compost area. If you designate a place for a compost pile, students can convert lunchroom and garden waste into a rich, soil-building ingredient and witness the wonder of decomposition. You could create a simple freestanding pile or make an enclosure from chicken wire, snow fencing, wooden pallets, concrete blocks, or lumber. Even an old garbage can with holes punched in it will suffice. Make sure the structure has openings for air circulation. If you have more than one pile, you can have some compost "cooking" while you add new ingredients to another batch. Also consider incorporating a worm composting setup into this area.

Signs. Consider using student-designed signs for the following purposes. Be sure to use weather-resistant materials.

Pumpkins
We planted big Pumpkins like the ones we see on Halloween. We decided to plant big pumpkins because we thought they would be fun to look at when we are all done. We also thought they would be interesting. On Halloween we can have all the seeds we want to eat. Also, the Indians used them as food, plus it's a cousin of squash.

Travis Taylor and Marcus Rini

- Identifying the project
- Communicating student feelings about the garden
- Publicizing sponsors
- Announcing hours and information on how to become involved
- Explaining unique garden features
- Providing rules and guidelines
- Labeling compost areas and providing instructions
- Identifying plants

Pond/wetland. Many teachers have discovered the value of aquatic ecosystems as dynamic teaching tools. Ponds can inspire explorations of plant/animal interactions and chemistry and offer a setting for reading, writing, and quiet reflection. But they do come with some safety concerns. Check with school administrators to see if there are any restrictions or safety precautions you should consider. If you don't have a natural pond or wetland, you'll need a flat open spot that gets at least 5 hours of sunlight a day. Unless you're renovating a preexisting pond, you will need some type of liner. You can install a preformed rigid plastic or fiberglass liner or a flexible one made from PVC or rubber. If you have limited space or simply want to start small, use a wooden half-barrel or some other type of tub. Students can research appropriate plants, fish, and other creatures, and create an environment to meet their basic needs.

Weather station. Consider cultivating keen weather watchers by incorporating a weather station into your garden. Students can monitor a variety of conditions and determine how different factors affect garden life. You might start simply by designing a rain gauge. Students can hang an old coffee can on a post, then mark a clear plastic straw with inches or centimeters. Once a week, they can insert the straw to the bottom of the can, put their thumb on the top, and withdraw it to read the depth of rainfall. Here are some other weather instruments you can purchase or make:

- Psychrometer (measures relative humidity)
- Barometer (measures air pressure)
- Hygrometer (measures humidity)
- Weather vane or wind sock (indicates wind direction)
- Ventemeter (measures wind speed)
- Minimum/maximum thermometer (measures temperature range)

Thinking Habitat?

Too often, students sit at their desks and learn about habitats and ecosystems thousands of miles away, while their schoolyard features a barren landscape of mown grass or asphalt. More and more schoolyards are being transformed into oases that support a diversity of animal life and inspire important environmental lessons. Many schoolyard stewards start simply, with a birdbath, a brush pile, or a few butterfly garden plants, for instance. Others have restored prairies or wetlands, or planted trees and shrubs for food and shelter.

If you want to invite more wildlife into your schoolyard, you should first discover who's already in the neighborhood and what types of features and conditions exist. Next, decide who you'd like to attract and learn what your intended guests need to thrive and reproduce. In general, the greater variety of plant types you have (trees, shrubs, perennials, annuals, and so on), the more wildlife you'll attract. Native plants are adapted to wildlife needs. Whether you're aiming for a schoolyard wildlife habitat or minihabitat, such as a pollinator or butterfly garden, here are some basic elements you'll need to consider:

Food. Consider what types of food wildlife need at different life stages. If you are trying to attract butterflies, for instance, you'll need to supply nectar plants for adult butterflies as well as plants with leaves that larvae feed on, such as parsley and milkweed. Small pollinators, such as wasps, go for herbs and other plants with lots of tiny flowers. Many birds need seeds and berries for sustenance.

Water. Birds, butterflies, frogs, and other wildlife need water. This can take the form of mud puddles, birdbaths, or shallow dishes or lids in the ground. If you do have space, a small pond will draw an even greater abundance of visitors.

Shelter and places to raise young. Trees and shrubs provide shelter and nesting sites for birds, wild grassy areas house small animals and insects such as grasshoppers, and fallen logs and brush piles provide habitat for reptiles. Some bees will even use upturned flowerpots for nesting.

The National Wildlife Federation (NWF) has excellent resources on designing and implementing habitats. Your school can also become certified as an NWF Schoolyard Habitat site. See page 53 for information.

Now we turn to the experts in designing schoolyard gardens and habitats: your colleagues and their young charges. We hope the following maps and project highlights will enlighten and inspire you as you learn how other educators have creatively engaged students in the planning and design process, staged multiyear projects, found funds and support, overcome dilemmas, and integrated the garden into the curriculum.

Edible Environments

From Garden to Cafeteria

"Last year our sixth graders raised vegetables and flowers to market," reports Santa Barbara, CA, teacher Roger Earles. "But this year our cafeteria is emphasizing a healthy school lunch program, so the students decided to donate most of the harvest to our own cafeteria. We've learned from experience that students are more willing to try new vegetables when they've helped nurture them."

Students first surveyed the school cafeteria staff to find out what types of garden produce they could use, then planted appropriate herb and vegetable gardens. Student-grown lettuce, carrots, radishes, and edible-pod peas now grace the salad bar. "We've had good support from our cafeteria staff," says Roger. "They encourage students to try foods by serving them in interesting ways—by creating a potato bar with a variety of toppings, for instance."

There's nothing like nurturing a lettuce plant or squash vine for inspiring proud young growers to, yes, taste vegetables. And there's nothing like the flavor of homegrown peas to keep them wanting more. With childhood obesity and diabetes on the rise, schoolyard vegetable gardens serve an ever more important role in nurturing lifelong healthful eating habits. There are other powerful reasons for growing vegetable gardens. They enable students to discover where food comes from and to explore edibles from other cultures. When garden food is donated to neighbors in need, students put a face on the issue of hunger and experience the power of taking action to improve their communities.

If you want students to be able to plant a garden and harvest it before school lets out for the summer, try to plant fast-growing vegetables, such as lettuce, peas, radishes, and carrots, in early spring (or winter if you're in the South). This is also a good practice if you don't have anyone to maintain the garden during the summer. If you want students to have vegetables to harvest when they return to school in the fall, plant those that require a long growing season, such as pumpkins, corn, tomatoes, and winter squash. The maps on page 16 feature layouts for a spring planting and full-season garden.

Are you hoping to cultivate lessons about environmental stewardship? Consider designing vegetable gardens that incorporate earth-friendly designs and techniques. For instance, include flowers and herbs that repel certain pests or attract insects that pollinate plants or prey on pests. Or rotate plantings each year to pave the way for good plant health. The maps and project highlights on pages 14 to18 offer inspiration.

Patchwork Quilt Garden

Don't be constrained by the classic image of long, straight rows of vegetables. Fourth, fifth, and sixth graders in Lansdale, PA, were inspired by a quilting project to design a vegetable garden resembling a quilt square. Each triangular section features a different group or family of plants that rotates position every year.

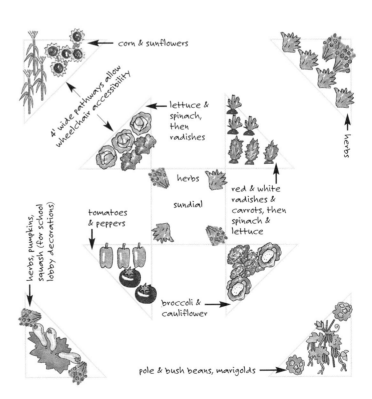

corn & sunflowers

4' wide pathways allow wheelchair accessibility

lettuce & spinach, then radishes

herbs

herbs

red & white radishes & carrots, then spinach & lettuce

sundial

herbs, pumpkins, squash (for school lobby decorations)

tomatoes & peppers

broccoli & cauliflower

pole & bush beans, marigolds

THE LUNCHBOX GARDEN CLUB
Rolling Hills Elementary School, Orlando, FL

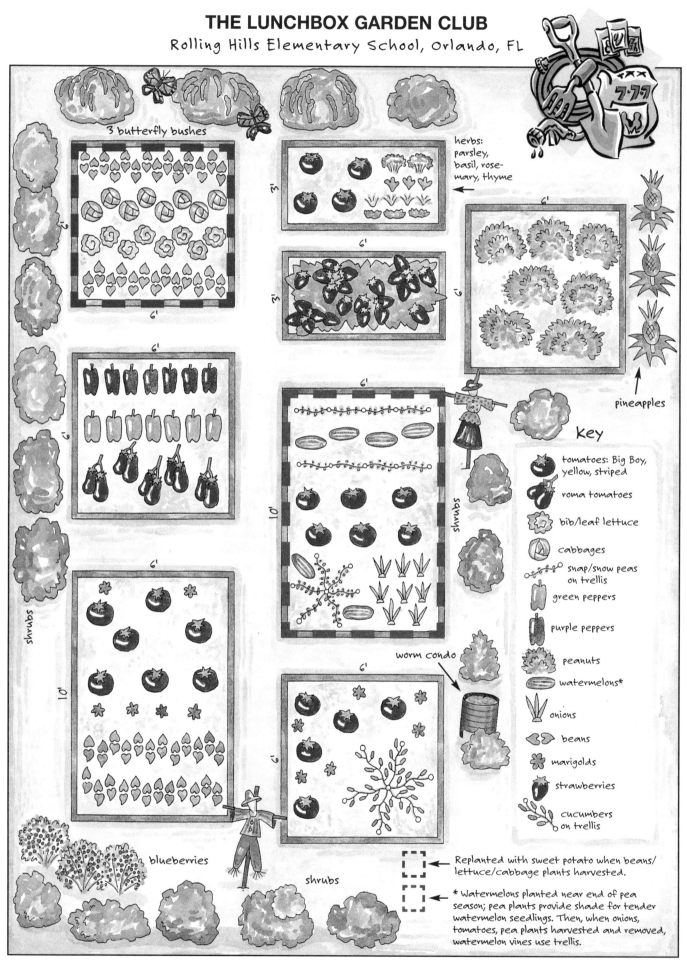

3 butterfly bushes

herbs: parsley, basil, rosemary, thyme

pineapples

worm condo

blueberries

shrubs

key

- tomatoes: Big Boy, yellow, striped
- roma tomatoes
- bib/leaf lettuce
- cabbages
- snap/snow peas on trellis
- green peppers
- purple peppers
- peanuts
- watermelons*
- onions
- beans
- marigolds
- strawberries
- cucumbers on trellis

Replanted with sweet potato when beans/lettuce/cabbage plants harvested.

* Watermelons planted near end of pea season; pea plants provide shade for tender watermelon seedlings. Then, when onions, tomatoes, pea plants harvested and removed, watermelon vines use trellis.

Cross-Grade Buddies Plant Garden Companions

Where: *Rolling Hills Elementary School, Orlando, FL*
Who: *Laurie Wedewer & Karen Redel, teachers*

How They Grew

"The garden has helped to blur grade levels by bringing teachers and students together into a group of 'farmers,'" explain Karen and Laurie. "Garden club members continue to brag about their green-thumb efforts, and we receive positive feedback from parents and teachers about the kids' academic and social skills." The teachers attribute improved behaviors to the fact that the youngsters had to work cooperatively to accomplish tasks and to the sense of ownership and responsibility that emerged. "Kids have bloomed from apathetic, reluctant learners to enthusiastic, inquisitive learners eager to reach out to the neighborhood," adds Karen.

"For a campus that has experienced a significant amount of vandalism, our garden seemed to create a level of reverence and respect," she says. "The club members model for a growing number of curious students how to look without touching, investigate without trampling, and smell without destroying."

When an ugly portable classroom was removed at Rolling Hills Elementary, an inner-city school with a high at-risk population, kindergarten teacher Karen Redel and fourth grade teacher Laurie Wedewer saw green. After all, their apartment-dwelling students assumed veggies only came in packages. With visions of a cross-grade food garden project that would offer fourth graders a chance to take leadership roles, the teachers established mentoring teams, each consisting of a fourth grade leader and several kindergarten "buddies."

Armed with fiction and nonfiction gardening books and Internet information, each team was challenged to create its vision of an ideal Florida garden. The partners had to design the layout (area and perimeter) of individual raised beds and mark vegetable plant locations. After all teams had presented their designs, the class discussed modifications and voted on a final garden layout.

Buddies Learn About Garden Companions

Through their research, the students discovered that certain vegetables "get along" better with each other, so the class planned its design to feature different arrangements of garden companions. For example, they learned that beans planted near lettuce could shade the heat-sensitive greens. Marigolds, which are said to be a natural pesticide, were partnered with tomatoes. Students relished the idea that onions could be juiced up into an organic bug repellent! "The kids discovered that if they planted watermelon seedlings toward the end of pea season, the pea plants would shade the tender seedlings," explains Karen. "Once the peas were removed, the watermelons used the pea trellis."

The partners learned that this plant buddy system—growing a variety of vegetables with different needs—can even help maintain healthy soil. The nutrient that one plant uses, in some cases, can be replenished by other plants. Corn, for instance, is a glutton for nitrogen, whereas peas and beans (with a little help from bacteria on their roots) can actually make nitrogen in the air available to other plants via the soil.

The teams worked together to clean the garden space, plot and stake the beds, and prepare the soil. Once they'd figured out when to plant each type of seed or seedling, they created and followed planting calendars. "The older kids took their roles very seriously and kept their buddies involved and focused on tasks," says Laurie.

Lunchbox Club Gives Back to the School and Community

Enthusiastic about their partnerships, the garden buddies were dismayed to realize that, come fall, they would move on to different grades and have to part ways. The solution? Creating an after-school Lunchbox Garden Club open to the diverse K-5 student body. (Club dues take the form of canned goods, which are donated to the local food bank.) In addition to maintaining the garden, club members taste-test produce before sending weekly harvests to the school cafeteria for salad bars, brewed mint iced tea, and more. They also use their newfound skills for community service projects, such as re-landscaping a neighboring church property, and for leading garden tours and lessons on seedling care for the school and community. Next, they have their sights set on creating how-to videos and introducing a garden mascot ("Corney"), who will challenge other classrooms with plant science trivia in preparation for spring assessments.

Two Basic Vegetable Garden Designs

If you and your students have decided on a vegetable garden, one thing you should consider is when you hope to harvest your bounty. Do you envision a spring salad garden? Do students look forward to pondering pumpkins or tasting tomatoes when they return to school in September? Perhaps you have a fall harvest festival planned.

Here, we share two sample vegetable garden layouts. The cool-season garden features plants that thrive in cool weather. Depending on your school calendar and region, and how early you get seeds and seedlings in the ground, you should be able to get a harvest from this garden before

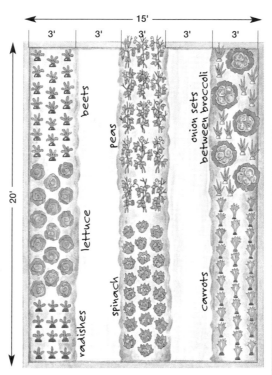

COOL-SEASON GARDEN

Planting Tips

Here are some general tips on planting and spacing the crops featured in these two gardens. Check seed packets for details. Your soil type, depth, and fertility, and a range of other factors affect how well plants do with different spacings. Invite your keen observers to keep tabs and experiment with their plantings.

spinach—rows 6"-12" apart
carrots—rows 8"-12" apart
beets—rows 8"-12" apart
radishes—rows about 4" apart
basil—rows 8"-18" apart
dill—rows 8" apart
nasturtiums—rows 8" apart
broccoli and cabbages—stagger rows to allow 2'-3' between plants
onions—plant sets (small bulbs you buy at garden centers) about 2" apart, between broccoli plants
peas—prior to planting, set up a trellis down the middle of a bed (for tall varieties) or poke small branches into the earth a few inches apart (for shorter varieties). Scatter peas in 4" swaths on either side of fencing.
lettuce—stagger plants every 8", or plant rows 8" apart and thin
corn—blocks of at least 3 rows, each 1' from the next
squash and pumpkins—4'-5' between plants
peppers and tomatoes—plants 2'-3' feet apart
cucumbers—put a trellis down the middle of wide bed and plant on either side
bean tepee—"plant" 4 poles as illustrated; plant 5-6 pole bean seeds around each and thin to 2-3 plants per pole

FULL-SEASON GARDEN

school lets out for the summer. You can raise these same crops in warm climates during fall and mild winters. The full-season garden includes a variety of cool- and warm-season plants that are fairly easy to grow in most areas. If you have help with summer garden maintenance, consider this mix of crops.

If you want to get a jump on the season, you can start seedlings of some crops indoors or buy them from a garden center or nursery. The easiest to grow indoors and transplant are broccoli, lettuce, tomatoes, and peppers. (Seed packets will tell you how early to start transplants and when to put them out.)

Organic Matters

Where: *Farnsworth Middle School, Schenectady, NY*
Who: *Mark Warford, teacher*

When students at the Farnsworth Middle School set out to start a garden, they examined the origins of our food and the agricultural system that produces it. "The students were concerned about the negative aspects of chemical-dependent agriculture, but determined to build a garden large enough to feed hundreds of people," says garden coordinator Mark Warford. The upshot? A 3/4-acre garden that features organic methods for "feeding" the soil, managing insect pests, and controlling weeds.

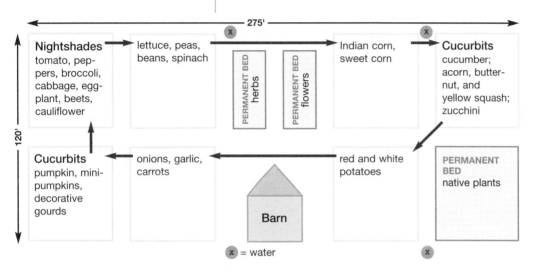

Indicates annual rotation of crops from one bed to another; green beds are permanent.

Rotating Veggies

The school's eight 45'x 45' plots generally host different families of plants. For instance, one area contains members of the nightshade family: tomatoes, peppers, and eggplants. Every year, the crops rotate into new plots, so each plant family or group occupies a certain section only once every three to four years. With this system, disease and pest problems associated with certain plants are less likely to get a foothold since things are always on the move.

"We base our decisions about how to organize the rotation and what to mix in each plot on several factors," explains Mark. For instance, crops that require a lot of nitrogen, such as corn or pumpkins, are typically followed by those that are considered "light feeders," like peas or onions. The gardeners also try to stagger root crops and leafy vegetables because their nutrient needs vary. Plants with small seeds that can be easily overtaken by weeds, such as carrots, follow larger crops, such as potatoes, that form a canopy and keep down weed growth.

Other Earth-friendly Techniques

Mark's students have discovered a host of other environmentally friendly approaches to maintaining a thriving garden. For instance, they plant cover crops such as clover or rye grass to cover bare soil. These "green manures" protect precious soil from erosion and, when turned back into the soil, add nutrient-rich organic matter. "Compost is one of the oldest and best soil additives, so we use a lot of it," says Mark. But his students haven't *just* relied on the tried and true. They've also had success with newer approaches, such as covering seedlings with lightweight fabric row covers. These let sun and rain in, but keep insects out. "We also stress conserving water and using renewable energy resources," explains Mark. To that end, they've set up a low-pressure drip irrigation system and used recycled plastic lumber to build raised beds, since it doesn't degrade or release harmful chemicals.

Spreading the Word

"Each day during the summer, students set up display boards explaining how organic agriculture meets plant needs without environmental and health risks," says Mark. As they conduct tours for community members, students challenge visitors to look at how the choices they make every day, such as the food they buy and energy they use, affect the environment. At the school's student-run farmer's market, visitors sample and purchase fresh organic vegetables. The income adds to the garden project's coffers, but it reflects just a fraction of the harvest. Students achieve their goal of feeding hundreds by donating the other 2,500 pounds of food harvested each year to soup kitchens and food pantries.

Nutritious Lessons: Snack Food Garden

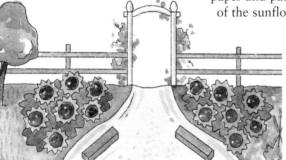

"**A** parent volunteer in my multiage class was appalled at the sugary snacks he saw the children eating during mid-morning break," reports Westminster, VT, teacher Irene Canaris. "As a farmer concerned about children's awareness of healthy eating, he offered to help us create a 'snack garden' that now nourishes the entire class throughout the school year." Irene's students plan and plant the garden each spring, and then with their families take turns caring for it during the summer. When children return in September, their first snack preparation adventure is harvesting and canning 85 pints of dilly beans. And that's just the beginning of the menu.

In math class, students multiply a recipe for pickle brine, then make crock-style cucumber pickles. "Children who initially refused to sample a fresh green pepper were clamoring for them after watching their friends eat them in class," reports Irene. Other snack foods include fresh cherry tomatoes, carrots, apples, and peas, and transformed vegetable treats such as carrot cake, carrot soup, roasted pumpkin seeds, baked potatoes, and mashed potatoes with rutabagas. To increase the quantity and variety of nutritious snacks, the class decided to write letters to local food businesses, describing the program and asking for donations. Locally produced cheddar cheese, apples, peanut butter, and crackers are now regularly featured foods.

But Irene's snack garden does more than just provide healthful foods: It also nourishes students' minds while supporting the curriculum. Students design garden maps, perform pH tests, take soil temperatures, and conduct investigations in their classroom GrowLab. "When our children are planning to triple a carrot cake recipe so 40 of them can eat it for a snack, 3 times $1/2$ cup of raisins becomes a meaningful math problem," explains Irene. "As they keep journal entries about their garden, they are becoming articulate writers. If they are sitting beside their garden on a warm September day with sketch paper and pastels, capturing the last yellow of the sunflowers, surely they are having an intimate aesthetic experience." (Motivated by her experiences, Irene is writing a standards-based food-garden curriculum for the early grades.)

Is the snack garden encouraging students to make healthier food choices? Here's some feedback straight from a parent: "When I pick my son up, inevitably the first unsolicited bit of information I get from him concerning his day is about what he had done in the garden and/or what he ate for snack. He has an awareness of the process of getting food to the table and also a wider range of food he will eat."

Note: We don't feature a specific design for a snack food garden, since any vegetable planting will do!

Where: *East Wing at Westminster Center School, Westminster, VT*
Who: *Irene Canaris & Diane Fuleihan, teachers*

Multipurpose Schoolyards

What image springs to mind when you hear the phrase "schoolyard transformation"? An asphalt expanse newly reclaimed by plush grass? A medly of raised beds where there once was litter? Birds and other wildlife encountering an inviting oasis? Imagine a mosaic of these images: a schoolyard with many facets and features that inspire discovery and diversion for the school and neighborhood communities. The following pages feature maps and stories of school growers who have moved beyond a single garden to integrate a variety of outdoor classroom elements: areas for recreation, habitat components, places to gather or study, artistic and cultural features, and more.

A multipurpose schoolyard doesn't have to unfold as part of a grand scheme. In fact, sometimes a sitewide design follows naturally on the heels of a small project. (Read about Mount Olive High School on page 23.) For instance, a butterfly garden could spark ideas for new habitat elements, such as trees and water for birds. In subsequent years, students might decide they need bird feeders, benches from which to observe feeding habits, and perhaps a nature trail, complete with signs, to observe woodland birds. And the schoolyard oasis grows, bit by bit.

> "Children study the history and geography of this country on blackboards; they see the maple leaf emblem on a flag; they read about the importance of red cedar, ferns, and wild berries to the people of this land, but now they can actually observe all of these things in a more natural setting."
>
> — *Illene Pevec, Grandview U'uqinak'uuh Community School (page 30)*

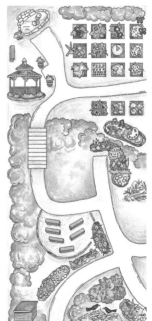

If it is possible and practical, try to develop a comprehensive vision up front in collaboration with students, teachers, custodians, and community members. This will enable you to build enthusiasm and motivation, lay the groundwork for raising funds and community support, and develop a thoughtful plan that works with your unique site. Once you have this ideal vision, you'll be better able to create a realistic timeline (one that considers available funds and other support) for completing the transformation.

Read on for inspiration and advice.

COURTYARD HABITAT
Lower Southampton Elementary School, Southampton, PA

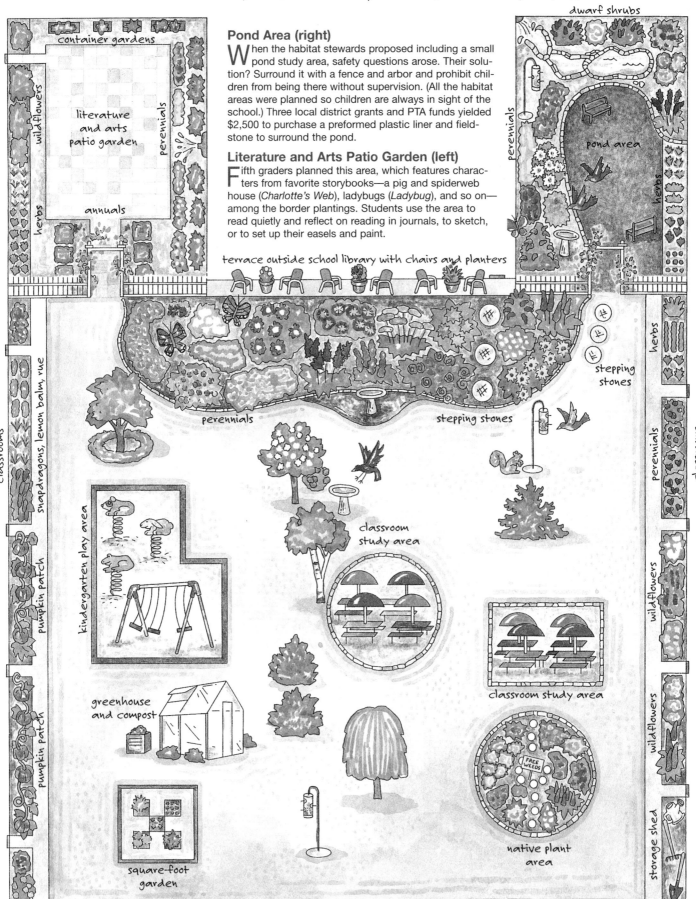

Pond Area (right)

When the habitat stewards proposed including a small pond study area, safety questions arose. Their solution? Surround it with a fence and arbor and prohibit children from being there without supervision. (All the habitat areas were planned so children are always in sight of the school.) Three local district grants and PTA funds yielded $2,500 to purchase a preformed plastic liner and fieldstone to surround the pond.

Literature and Arts Patio Garden (left)

Fifth graders planned this area, which features characters from favorite storybooks—a pig and spiderweb house (*Charlotte's Web*), ladybugs (*Ladybug*), and so on—among the border plantings. Students use the area to read quietly and reflect on reading in journals, to sketch, or to set up their easels and paint.

container gardens

literature and arts patio garden

wildflowers

perennials

herbs

annuals

dwarf shrubs

perennials

pond area

herbs

terrace outside school library with chairs and planters

perennials

stepping stones

herbs

perennials

stepping stones

classrooms

snapdragons, lemon balm, rue

classrooms

classroom study area

classroom study area

kindergarten play area

pumpkin patch

pumpkin patch

greenhouse and compost

FREE WEEDS

native plant area

wildflowers

wildflowers

square-foot garden

storage shed

Courtyard Allure

Where: *Lower Southampton Elementary School, Southampton, PA*
Who: *Joanne Bauer, teacher and habitat coordinator*

Garnering Funds and Donations

How do you get what you need to bring your vision to life? These habitat gardeners used a range of strategies. Staff members wrote and received grants from the National Gardening Association, a local education foundation, the school district, and Ames Department stores.

Student entrepreneurs took another tack. They held bake sales, sold daffodil bulbs, and created and marketed first-aid kits and "Habitat Hannah" dolls (wearing paper clothing with gardening and nature designs). The school PTA agreed to establish a "habitat account" to provide funds for plants and new projects. Parents and local businesses have donated and discounted plants and other materials. "As businesses have seen the school's commitment to the project, it has become much easier to solicit donations," Joanne explains. "We have found that the more you document your progress and the more you can show what you have accomplished, the more people are willing to help you with what you need. It is important to show that you have made a serious commitment to completing and maintaining the project."

"I was first inspired to have the kids turn our enclosed courtyard into a garden and habitat when I attended the Children's Garden Symposium a few years back," says third grade teacher Joanne Bauer. "The ideas and resources from colleagues and experts got my creative juices flowing." Knowing that a schoolyard transformation would require *lots* of allies, Joanne invited the PTA president to go with her the following year. This strategy helped open the PTA's eyes to the possibilities, and paid off handsomely down the road!

When staff, students, and parents in the K-5 school sat down to brainstorm ideas for a living courtyard, they first considered some of the project's goals: to build school/community relations and seek ways to help the environment, for instance. Then they dug in. "First an interested group mapped out the area on graph paper to see what features already exist and decided what we wanted to leave," says Joanne. Next, the designers learned about basic habitat needs—food, water, shelter, and places to raise young—and explored how they could incorporate them into the courtyard. Finally, they marked on their map the features they hoped to add, such as trees, flower beds, a pond, and birdbaths. "As we created our vision, we made sure to get the custodial staff on our side early on!" says Joanne.

Pondering Priorities

"Our map revealed an ideal, completed project, but we knew that it might take years to get there," says Joanne. (In fact, it took nine years to create the multipurpose courtyard you see here.) "So we chose priorities that we could accomplish with our current resources." Each year, the habitat stewards selected one new project or area to work on. Joanne explains that as the years went by and people became aware of the emerging habitat, a growing cadre of volunteers helped them take on larger projects and maintain the site. A signup sheet goes home in June and families volunteer for one day during the summer to water and weed the gardens, record interesting observations in a journal, and enjoy whatever bounty is ready to harvest. During the school year, a before- and after-school Kids' Club and various classrooms "adopt" areas to maintain.

"I urge other teachers considering a schoolyard garden or habitat to start with small, doable pieces," says Joanne. "You might begin with a few bushes, a small variety of plants that attract butterflies, and a bird feeder, and then tackle bigger projects as you get funding, donations of materials and labor, and advice from local businesses, landscapers, garden clubs, garden centers, and others."

Bringing the Curriculum Alive

"I have seen many students become more excited about reading and writing by using the outdoor habitat as a motivational tool," says Joanne. She and colleagues are putting together a handbook of activities that address the Pennsylvania State Assessment standards to use in the outdoor setting: pond studies, water-quality testing, yarn dyeing with garden plants, color and shape searches, and presentation of a habitat guide talk, to name a few. As part of a new club, Children's Environmental Outreach, which was inspired by the project, kids take what they've learned to educate others about how to help protect habitats. The group, which meets monthly, has helped build a wildflower garden area at a local park and is creating a PowerPoint presentation about the schoolyard habitat to share with others.

A WALK ON THE WILD SIDE

Mt. Olive School, Mt. Olive, NJ

cultivated side

wild side

brush pile

rotting logs

existing tree copse

pond and wetlands

nesting boxes

study area

berry patch

native berry bushes along split-rail fence

gate

succession area

nesting boxes

compost

storage shed

bird feeder

herb garden

Dutch bulbs

native perennials

butterfly garden

grass plots

sundial and weather study area

vegetable garden

erosion control area

bird feeder

Surveying Succession

The amorphous shape of the Succession Area, dictated by available space, meshes well with other features on the garden's wild side. Nancy's students rototilled the area to remove the existing vegetation and then left it to go to seed. "As with natural succession, we hope this area will evolve from weeds and grasses to shrubs and eventually deciduous and coniferous saplings. It's a natural progression that will take time," explains Nancy. Along the way, her students will patiently witness and document how a piece of natural land recovers when it is left to its own devices.

Exploring Erosion

Divided into equal rectangular sections, the Erosion Control Area is built into a small slope. The first section contains only soil. In different years, the other sections are planted with native weeds, cultivated grasses, or mulched flowers and small shrubs. At the low end of the area, 5-inch-deep pans collect soil from each section as it washes away during rainstorms. Students determine how effective the different planting schemes are at controlling erosion by measuring the amount of soil collected in the pans, observing how each section erodes, and documenting which section retains the most soil.

Grasping Grasses

The rectangular Grass Plot is divided into four equal sections. Nancy's students sow a different type of grass in each one: "lawn" grass in the first, native wild grass in the second, and prairie grasses (e.g., little and big bluestem) in the last two. Students use the plot to draw comparisons between wild and domesticated grasses. For instance, they trim each grass type and document how it responds, and they measure height until each grass type goes to seed. (Big bluestem can reach 6 feet in height!) Nancy's students also record observations on the stems, leaves, seedheads, and root structures of each.

A Walk on the Wild Side

Where: *Mt. Olive High School, Mt. Olive, NJ*
Who: *Nancy Sklavos-Gillett, teacher*

Getting the Word Out

Students in Nancy's special-needs classroom have carefully documented every aspect of their schoolyard habitat project. And they love to share this information. They've been recognized in two local newspapers and on a televised news brief. The habitat is registered with the National Gardening Association, The National Wildlife Federation, and the New Jersey Alliance for Environmental Education. The students have even networked with an Australian educator and newsletter publisher who created and maintains their schoolyard habitat Web site (*www.virtual-teacher.com.au/schooly/schooly.html*).

A corner of Nancy Sklavos-Gillett's classroom is dedicated to the study of ecology. She found that, despite being hands-on, activities such as forcing bulbs and planting seeds in the classroom were too abstract for her special-needs students. Now, to make learning more concrete, Nancy incorporates the woodlands surrounding Mt. Olive High School into their ecological studies.

Learning by Design

It all began with a perennial garden. As soon as the school administration granted planting space, Nancy's students began using the Internet to research potential donors. They developed math skills by creating budgets for supplies and honed language arts skills by writing letters to local merchants requesting donations. In the midst of organizing and cataloging donated seeds, plants, and tools, students wrote personalized thank-you notes. Finally, they prepared the garden soil, relocated existing plants, and planted a flurry of flowers.

Once the perennial garden was complete, the class went to work on the rest of the site. Using a grid system, each student created a map of the area. The master plan, which includes a "wild" and a "cultivated" side, incorporates design features from each of their maps. The wild side, replete with ferns, mosses, jack-in-the-pulpits, and native wildflowers, encourages investigations of local fauna and flora. Student-built bird feeders, nesting boxes, and birdbaths adorn the area. Rock piles, brush piles, and rotting logs provide habitat for small mammals, reptiles, and insects and launch explorations into decomposition, the food chain, and habitat requirements. Students can observe natural succession in the area where they rototilled a plot to remove the vegetation. As it becomes reestablished, students use plant and animal field guides to identify newcomers.

In contrast, the cultivated side includes vegetable, herb, and butterfly gardens and some experimental plots. A fenced compost pile; an erosion control area; and a weather station equipped with a rain gauge, thermometer, and sundial complete the picture. Students conduct experiments, take measurements, and record observations in the grass plots to compare domesticated and native species.

Measuring Results

"The habitat is a vehicle that is used to apply the curriculum standards mandated by the state for each student as well as the varied Individual Education Plan (IEP) requirements," explains Nancy. Each student maintains a portfolio, which is an excellent assessment tool, throughout the year and documents time spent and tasks completed in the garden. Students also use the portfolios when they pursue employment opportunities. "The students have acquired skills in procedures, communications, and relationships," Nancy explains. "And they have learned life skills necessary for their transition from school to work. These special-needs students have earned support from the school administration, other students and teachers, the ground crew, community members, local and national merchants, local and national organizations, the press, and media."

PLAYGROUND IN A GARDEN
Cardinal Bernardin Early Childhood Center, Chicago, IL

butterfly garden

ramp to school buildings

flower garden runs along fence

mulched path

jungle gym surrounded by wood chips; area enclosed with plastic edging

vegetable and sunflower house maze

vegetable garden

log ring with mulch

sandbox with wooden frame

school building: windows overlooking garden are three stories high

Pond Dilemma

The original Playground in a Garden design included a stream and a pond, as illustrated in this map. The children at Cardinal Bernardin wanted to add toads and fish to this schoolyard wildlife component. But administrators were concerned about liability issues. Ann proposed a compromise. Now, instead of a pond, a wetland—complete with a boardwalk and rowboat—adds an aquatic element to this kid-friendly schoolyard habitat.

Plant Selection for Young Kids

Butterfly garden
Black-eyed Susan
Coneflower
Coreopsis
Cosmos
Daylily
Johnny jump-up
Liatris
Bee balm
New England aster
Queen Anne's lace

Vegetable garden
Broccoli
Cauliflower
Corn
Pepper
Pumpkin
Tomato

Flower garden
Chrysanthemum
Clematis
Daylily
Loosestrife
Obedient plant
Rose
Sunflower

Playground in a Garden

Where: *Cardinal Bernardin Early Childhood Center, Chicago, IL*
Who: *Ann Marischen, garden coordinator*

Overcoming Urban Issues

With an alley to the east and a parking lot to the south, the Playground in a Garden is an oasis in a sea of asphalt. Ann reports that most kids who come to the center have no green spaces of their own. She has learned some hard lessons gardening in this urban environment. Take, for example, the time the group hung feeders to attract birds to the schoolyard. When rats from the alley began frequenting the garden along with the birds, the feeders were removed. Now the kids grow sunflowers to attract goldfinches and cardinals instead.

When they dug into the soil, the staff discovered that the property had once been used as a landfill. To steer clear of the broken bricks, cement, and other refuse, Ann suggested using slightly raised growing beds.

Although the school building has been damaged by graffiti and broken windows, the garden has never been vandalized. In fact, the garden gate has no lock, so neighborhood kids often play there after hours. "Maybe by allowing the neighbors to come in and keeping it well maintained we have earned a certain amount of respect," Ann reflects.

"I usually just think something sounds fun for the kids and we go for it," says Ann Marischen, the garden coordinator at Cardinal Bernardin Early Childhood Center. So far, so good. By taking into account the interests and special needs of little ones, Ann and her colleagues have successfully transformed a 125' x 50' schoolyard into the "Playground in a Garden," a place where kids ages 3 to 8 are flourishing.

A Safe Place to Grow

"We knew we had to make it possible for a 3-year-old to explore the garden without destroying it," says Ann. So she watched how kids used the existing space and learned that the children liked to observe bugs and flowers up close. She also learned that every tree represented a safe base in games of tag, making it unfeasible to grow anything underneath them. Ann envisioned a network of stepping-stone paths and narrow beds that would keep everything within the reach of small hands. Instead of plants with tempting berries or crab apples, the garden would sport pumpkins, sunflowers, and other children's favorites.

Ann's careful observations paid off. In one corner of the schoolyard, an organic vegetable garden supports a flurry of year-round activity. The children plant seeds in the classroom and transplant them into the garden. During the summer, they harvest and deliver vegetables to the food pantry next door. When hungry rabbits munched on their carrots, the kids welcomed the furry visitors by fencing off a few vegetables and planting parsley for them. In the fall, the kids build scarecrows; carve pumpkins; and collect, dry, and package seeds to sell at the school carnival.

The children also listen to stories, eat snacks, and practice walking on "balance beams" in the log storytelling ring. The native annuals in the butterfly garden "stand up to a lot of hands-on (and feet-in) observation as they attract wonderful butterflies and bees that the children love," explains Ann. A memorial rose garden blossoms along the fence to keep curious fingers from getting pricked. A large grassy area and a sandbox invite good, old-fashioned child play. With hopes of attracting dragonflies, toads, and fish, the gardeners have started a wetland, complete with boardwalk and rowboat, in another corner of the schoolyard.

Encouraging Enthusiasm

"We challenge ourselves every year to try something new to stimulate the children's curiosity," explains Ann. "Last year, the vegetable garden was laid out in a maze with a sunflower house in the center. This year we are experimenting with different Three Sisters combinations." One year, the children worked with Ann to brainstorm materials they could use to create a miniature version of their garden. Their model is still proudly displayed in the entrance to the school building.

"The kids have learned how to spend time observing and appreciating all the little things that do their jobs to make a natural habitat work—the bees, the worms, the birds, the seeds, the rain," explains Ann. The only thing she would change is the placement of the jungle gym. "If we had known in the beginning what our garden would become, it would have been nice to have the jungle gym at one end of the yard instead of in the middle," she says. Although the sewer system dictated this placement, Ann would recommend separating the "loud" side of the schoolyard from the "quiet" side, if possible.

THE CHILDREN'S GARDEN
Brookpark Memorial School, Brook Park, OH

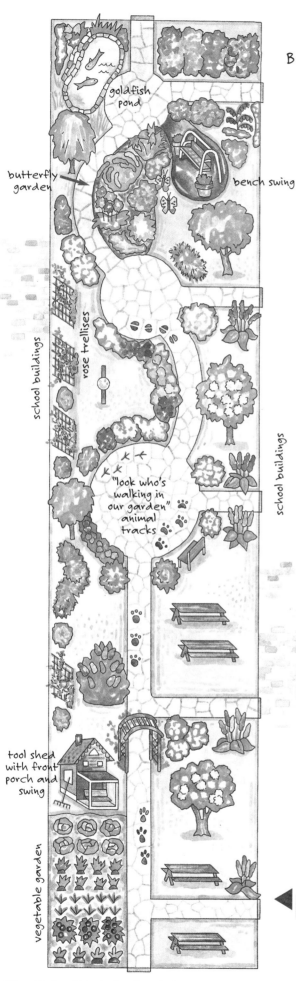

goldfish pond

butterfly garden

bench swing

rose trellises

school buildings

"look who's walking in our garden" animal tracks

tool shed with front porch and swing

vegetable garden

school buildings

the school courtyard before its transformation (looking west)

the same courtyard, after transformation (still looking west)

N

Butterfly Garden Plants

Aster	Phlox
Bee balm	Purple coneflower
Black-eyed Susan	Santolina
Butterfly bush	Scabiosa
Chrysanthemum	Sedum
Daylily	Yarrow

Landscape Plants

Arborvitae	Holly
Astilbe	Hosta
Azalea	Iris
Bleeding heart	Juniper
Boxwood	Lady's mantle
Burning bush	Lilac
Chrysanthemum	Mugo pine
Clematis	Rhododendron
Climbing rose	Spirea
Daylily	Weigela
Dwarf Alberta spruce	Yew

The Great Courtyard Makeover

Where: *Brookpark Memorial School, Brook Park, OH*
Who: *Rosemary Johnston and Denise Krane, teachers*

Valuing Volunteers

Rosemary and Denise know that without volunteers, the school's dreams for The Children's Garden would never have been realized. To show their appreciation, they held well-planned workdays, provided lots of good food, and sent many thank-you notes. "The best part of our project is seeing the kindness and generosity of so many people as we make life more beautiful for our children," says Denise.

She offers these other tips for keeping volunteers happy and coming back:

- Ask individuals to become involved by making phone calls or sending personal invitations.

- Show appreciation often by sending student-created thank-you notes or gifts and by recognizing volunteers through news articles or awards ceremonies.

- Understand why volunteers have become involved and try to meet their needs.

- Hold training sessions to make sure volunteers feel capable and competent at the tasks you assign.

It used to be that when students at Brookpark Memorial School looked out the window, they saw a rundown courtyard. Once there was a straight cement sidewalk. Now there is a curved red path. Once there was no place to sit. Now there is a bench swing from which students can watch six resident goldfish swimming in a pond. Students never used to visit the courtyard. Now they never want to leave.

Starting Small

Brookpark Memorial has two interior courtyards, one large and one small. After almost two years of visiting other school gardens, teachers Rosemary Johnston and Denise Krane, along with a core group of staff members, decided to start simply. They would renovate the small courtyard first to get their feet wet before transforming the larger courtyard into a learning laboratory.

If their ultimate success could be gauged by instantaneous excitement, they were off to a fruitful start. "The entire school got involved," explains Rosemary. Students pulled weeds, tamed overgrown plants, removed stones, and planted annuals. Staff members and parents hauled wheelbarrows full of soil into the garden. Families donated perennials, staff members donated hanging baskets, and students donated homemade and store-bought bird feeders.

To keep the momentum, the school community immediately began planning the learning lab. Each class chose one student to be on the garden committee that met with Rosemary and Denise to share dreams for the courtyard. The assistant supervisor for the buildings and grounds department donated his time and horticultural knowledge to translate these dreams into a master plan. When the master plan was presented to the rest of the school community, money started flowing in.

"By tackling the small courtyard first, we were able to form a core group of people who had a reputation for doing things well," says Denise. "As a result, when we approached the Lions Club and PTA, both groups were glad to help because they knew we'd get the job done."

Thinking Big

Before long, the parents of a garden committee member came forward. Owners of a concrete business, they offered to donate the labor to remove 70,000 pounds of straight sidewalk and replace it with a curved red path. The school borrowed large rubber animal track stamps from the nearby Metropark. Before the new pathway dried, raccoon, mice, deer, and duck footprints were stamped into it. Preschool students created a guide to the tracks called *Look Who's Walking in Our Garden*, with pictures and a description of each creature. Then came the pond and the vegetable and butterfly gardens. Next on the schedule: a tool shed designed, built, and painted with donated labor.

A constant flurry of activity now fills the once-abandoned courtyard. Classes are held next to the butterfly garden. Students harvest and donate produce from the vegetable garden. Guidance counselors meet with students, and reward lunches are celebrated at the picnic tables. Other project outcomes? One youngster sums it up simply: "This garden has made our dreams come true!"

OAK ACRES
Oak Elementary School, Bartlett, TN

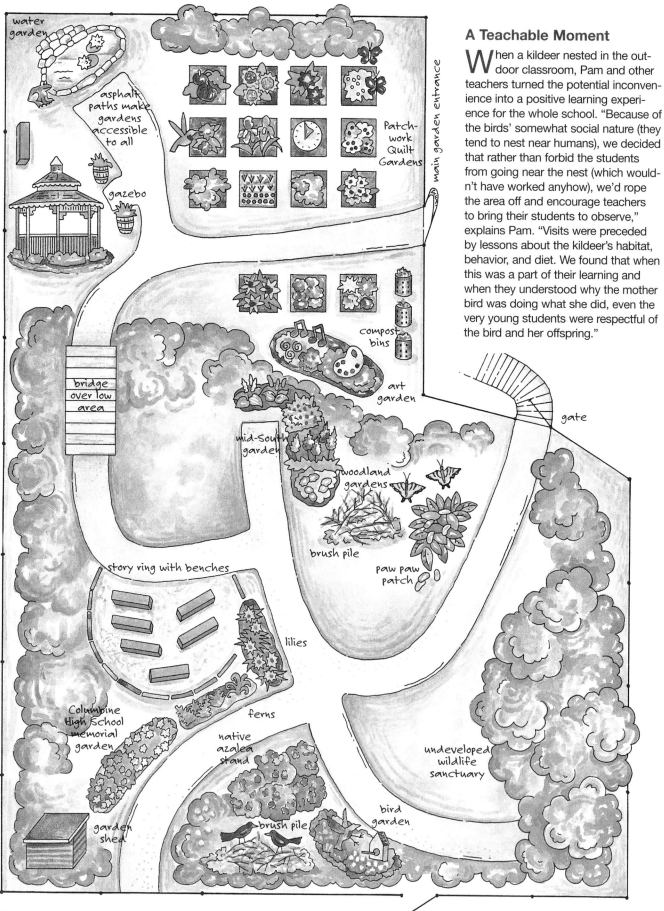

water garden

asphalt paths make gardens accessible to all

gazebo

Patch-work Quilt Gardens

main garden entrance

bridge over low area

compost bins

art garden

mid-South garden

woodland gardens

brush pile

paw paw patch

story ring with benches

lilies

Columbine High School memorial garden

ferns

native azalea stand

undeveloped wildlife sanctuary

garden shed

brush pile

bird garden

gate

A Teachable Moment

When a kildeer nested in the outdoor classroom, Pam and other teachers turned the potential inconvenience into a positive learning experience for the whole school. "Because of the birds' somewhat social nature (they tend to nest near humans), we decided that rather than forbid the students from going near the nest (which wouldn't have worked anyhow), we'd rope the area off and encourage teachers to bring their students to observe," explains Pam. "Visits were preceded by lessons about the kildeer's habitat, behavior, and diet. We found that when this was a part of their learning and when they understood why the mother bird was doing what she did, even the very young students were respectful of the bird and her offspring."

From Wasteland to Wonderland

Where: *Oak Elementary School, Bartlett, TN*
Who: *Pam Irving, Oak ACRES chairwoman*

Overcoming Obstacles

Despite their accomplishments, Pam admits that the road hasn't always been smooth. The biggest obstacle was learning to work with the county school system and city government. "It is not that either of these systems placed hurdles in our way. The fact that we did not understand how either of these functioned with regard to an outdoor classroom created difficulties in our fulfilling requirements, like how tall a fence could be and how close it could be to the street," she explains. "This obstacle was overcome through cooperation and a concerted effort on our part to learn the proper procedures and channels through which work is accomplished."

Another hurdle centers on the anxiety that some teachers feel about working in the outdoor classroom with students. "Some fear that they don't know how to use it, while others fear spiders and snakes," says Pam. She hopes that education, eventually in the form of inservice training, will assuage any trepidation.

It was only fitting for the parents, teachers, and administrators at Oak Elementary School to transform a section of the schoolyard from a construction dump site into 2 acres of open meadow and woodland. After all, the school's motto is "leave every place a little better than you found it." In 1987, Oak ACRES (Area Conserved as a Resource for Environmental Study) became one of the first outdoor classrooms in Tennessee. Before long, an area that had once been cluttered with broken toilets and chunks of concrete sported a log story ring and rambling trails.

Regaining Momentum

When the core group of founders moved on, Oak ACRES lay unused for many years. The PTA, concerned about the neglected site, dedicated part of its budget to fencing the area to deter vandals and prepare for the eventual construction of a pond. "At that point, development snowballed," recalls Oak ACRES Chairwoman Pam Irving.

As a first step, the school had 12'x12' plots (15 in all) tilled to create the "Patchwork Quilt Gardens." Teachers from every grade level sponsored gardens. Each class chose a theme and was responsible for designing, planting, and maintaining its own plot. Through the years, themes have ranged from Tennessee Treasures to a cactus garden. "Each is as unique as the individual patches in a handmade quilt," says Pam.

Enthusiasm for the Patchwork Quilt Gardens inspired the creation of eight woodland gardens. The short distance between the woodland and meadow habitats enables students to investigate the different plants and animals that occupy each. They can dig even deeper thanks to a PTA-supported outreach program. Naturalists are invited to visit the school and teach students about plants, wildlife, natural resources, and conservation. A small pond invites students to explore the life cycles of amphibians, fish, and aquatic plants. A bird sanctuary, featuring bird feeders and berry-producing shrubs, entices feathered creatures, and brush piles and evergreen trees provide year-round shelter for other wildlife.

Next, the school purchased a gazebo. A popular gathering place for teachers and students, this structure makes an ideal classroom. Teachers like to engage half their class in the garden while the other half quietly reflects in the gazebo with sketchpads and library books. Whiskey barrels located on either side of the gazebo

entrance overflow with ivy topiaries, pansies, and marigolds. At one time, these containers enabled handicapped students to garden. Now, a new bridge and 450 feet of paved paths make the entire outdoor classroom accessible to wheelchairs.

Fostering Flexibility

Looking back, Pam describes the site design as serendipitous. "Even though we laid out a long-term plan in the very beginning, as we learned over time what our teachers wanted and didn't want, used and didn't use, we adapted the plan to fit." They are still adapting. Future elements include an after-school program, an arboretum, an improved plant- and tree-marking system, and a vermiculture program.

SPIRIT OF NATURE SCHOOLYARD

Grandview U'uqinak'uuh Community School, Vancouver, BC

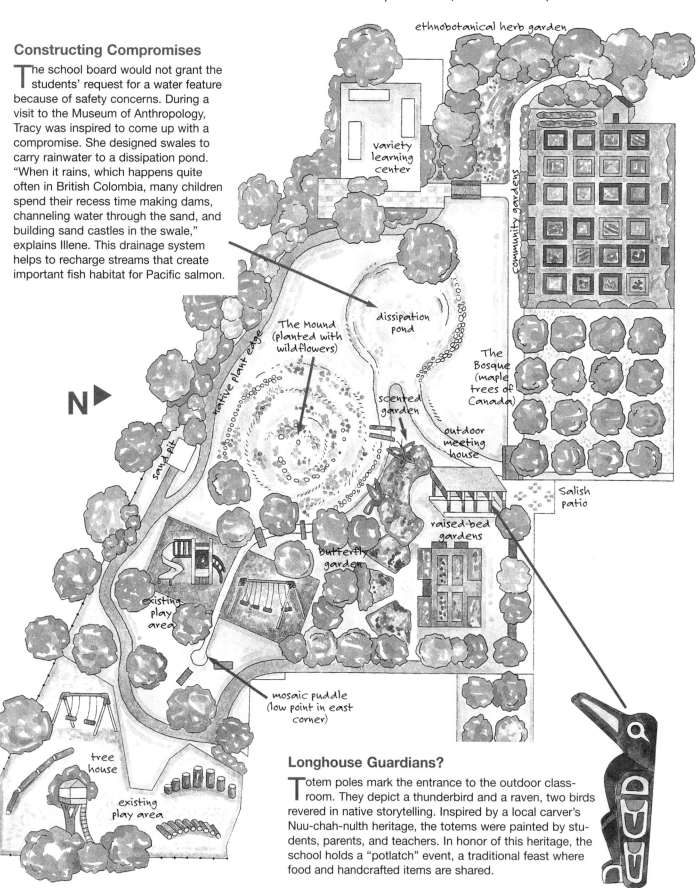

ethnobotanical herb garden

variety learning center

Community gardens

The Mound (planted with wildflowers)

dissipation pond

The Bosque (maple trees of Canada)

native plant edge

scented garden

outdoor meeting house

Salish patio

sand pit

N▶

raised-bed gardens

butterfly garden

existing play area

mosaic puddle (low point in east corner)

tree house

existing play area

Constructing Compromises

The school board would not grant the students' request for a water feature because of safety concerns. During a visit to the Museum of Anthropology, Tracy was inspired to come up with a compromise. She designed swales to carry rainwater to a dissipation pond. "When it rains, which happens quite often in British Colombia, many children spend their recess time making dams, channeling water through the sand, and building sand castles in the swale," explains Illene. This drainage system helps to recharge streams that create important fish habitat for Pacific salmon.

Longhouse Guardians?

Totem poles mark the entrance to the outdoor classroom. They depict a thunderbird and a raven, two birds revered in native storytelling. Inspired by a local carver's Nuu-chah-nulth heritage, the totems were painted by students, parents, and teachers. In honor of this heritage, the school holds a "potlatch" event, a traditional feast where food and handcrafted items are shared.

Creating a Cultural Connection

Where: *Grandview U'uqinak'uuh Community School, Vancouver, BC*
Who: *Illene Pevec and Tracy Penner, garden visionaries*

Plant Choices

Tracy explains that the school team selected plants that would enhance the ecology and the cultural and educational value of the site. Fifty percent of the community is of First Nations descent, so the garden incorporates plants used by their ancestors. And by choosing a variety of native plants for the butterfly and hummingbird garden, wild bird habitat, and other areas, the team helps preserve biodiversity in an urban environment.

These are the criteria the design team used to select plants for the schoolyard:

1. Plants that support native animal life.

2. Plants that have traditional value to aboriginal people.

3. Plants that are suited to the microclimate, for instance, those with tolerance to summer drought and winter moisture.

The school's name, Grandview U'uqinak'uuh Community School, reflects the region's rich cultural heritage. Now, the "Spirit of Nature" schoolyard proudly does the same. Graduate education student Illene Pevec and landscape architecture student Tracy Penner brought together students, parents, teachers, and community members to turn an underused, muddy, 1-acre field into a multigenerational, award-winning garden that celebrates and preserves local cultural history.

Building a Community of Knowledge

In search of a graduate research project, Illene turned to Grandview U'uqinak'uuh Community School with the idea of developing a garden. After proposing the idea to administrators and conducting extensive research, she wrote a grant to the Parks Department. Illene knew she needed help. Tracy, who was finishing her degree in landscape architecture, was interested. Equipped with practical knowledge and bountiful enthusiasm, the two women crafted a plan.

First, Tracy and Illene banded together with the school principal and a lead teacher who would facilitate meetings with other Grandview teachers, staff, and students. They invited several potential advisors to participate, including landscape architects, a native plant expert, an architect, and the grounds supervisor. Next, they conducted a site inventory. This included reviewing sewer, drainage, and underground utility plans; old maps; school architecture drawings; and neighborhood aerial photographs to compile information on soil type, water availability, and weather conditions.

Recognizing the importance of including students, teachers, parents, and other community members in the design process, Tracy and Illene held several workshops. The student workshops came first. Working in groups of six, students created maps representing how they used the schoolyard and built three-dimensional models of their dream gardens using sand trays and natural objects. "Almost every student requested a stream, pond, and waterfall," recalls Tracy. At the end of the workshop, students went home with surveys for their parents to complete.

Next, the two champions held separate teacher/staff and community planning workshops. At Grandview, the sessions were part of the school meeting agenda. To advertise the community workshop, the two sent home notices with students and hung posters around the neighborhood. Each workshop began with a brainstorming session on important aspects of a schoolyard, issues to overcome, and garden design. Teams were asked to prioritize the brainstormed list. Finally, the whole group conducted a "hot-dotting" exercise to vote for their preferences. Each participant received seven dots representing $1,000 each to place next to the features on which they would prefer to spend their money. The tabulated results informed the final design. Lacking postage funds, the organizers hand-delivered surveys to neighbors to solicit additional input.

Tracy used the input to draft three plans for the schoolyard. After presenting them to the grounds supervisor, she revised and presented them to Grandview teachers and staff. Finally, she consolidated the three plans into one master plan and took it to the school board for approval.

A Design That Celebrates Culture

"Every child, staff member, and interested community member participated in envisioning and designing the school grounds," recalls Illene. The site, as a result, reflects the neighborhood population. The area, now densely populated and crowded with low-income housing, once belonged to three First Nations groups: the Musqueam, the Burrard, and the Squamish. Fifty percent of the community is of First Nations heritage, though many are disconnected from the history and culture of their ancestors. The plant life and architectural design of the Spirit of Nature schoolyard reconnect students and community members to the people who influenced the character of their surroundings.

The covered outdoor classroom, designed in the style of a traditional Musqueam longhouse, sits in the center of the schoolyard with the entrances facing north and south. This orientation was preferred because it takes full advantage of the sun yet is protected from winter winds. Fitting up to 40 people, it is "a community gathering place for outdoor learning and celebration," says Tracy. It provides a sheltered place to read, conduct classes, watch performances, and hold community celebrations. In fact, chiefs from all three First Nations attended the longhouse dedication ceremony, in which students participated in traditional cultural activities.

The Coast Salish (a group that includes the Musqueam) are known for their skillful weaving. Recognizing this as a dying art form, the University of British Colombia established the Museum of Anthropology to preserve and display coastal arts and crafts. Tracy and the students spent hours at the museum, researching and gaining inspiration for the garden design. During a field trip there, sixth and seventh graders studied traditional weaving patterns. They designed their own patterns on graph paper and then used these patterns to lay bricks in the schoolyard patio.

At the other end of the garden site, a concrete wall (not pictured on map) stood in stark contrast to the lush green life springing up around it. "We knew we needed to somehow give life to that huge concrete wall, and the theme should somehow connect the school, garden, and community," explains Tracy. A local artist met with students and brainstormed ideas about what lives in and around rivers in British Colombia. He incorporated their ideas into a mural and transferred it to the wall. Students painted the "River of Life" mural, which now prominently illustrates the importance of water as a source of life.

Discovering People/Plant Connections

"Information about the traditional use of native plants by aboriginal people in this region has almost been lost," explains Illene. "The idea behind the ethnobotanical garden is to encourage elders who know about these plants to share their information with others." A group of native elders and young adults planned this garden, and teachers and students planted it. Now families can come to the schoolyard to learn the names and uses of indigenous plants from First Nations herbalists. Illene has even developed curriculum materials to help students learn about these plants' uses and folklore.

The personal impact that this project has had on students is as important as what it's taught them about their cultural heritage. "They have seen the real, physical results of planning and carrying out their plans and felt the pride that comes with such success," explains Tracy. "They have transformed their soggy, barren field into a vital neighborhood backyard."

Thematic Garden Snapshots

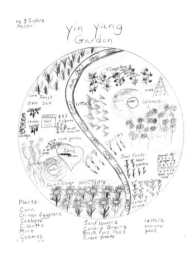

Kids Heal the Earth

After September 11, 2001, the Children's Discovery Garden in Burlington, VT, held a Kid's Garden Design Contest. The challenge? Design an 18-foot-wide circular garden that reflects a theme of "peace and healing of the Earth." Sisters Marcella, Elena, and Bianca imagined a plot shaped like a yin-yang symbol, which represents harmony and balance. A family brainstorm session helped the planting plan unfold: caring carrots; a sunflower sanctuary; the Native American companions corn, beans, and squash; cosmos flowers to represent the harmonious universe, and more. The design was the hands-down vote getter when displayed along with others at a local flower show. "The organizers of this unique project, who truly value kids' ideas, asked my kids how they could help bring their plans to life," says the girls' mother, Julia.

I magine the potential for motivating students and inspiring research and investigations when you have a theme around which to weave your garden project. Some school gardeners devote one or more beds to unique themes (historical herbs or dye and fiber plants, for instance). Others create entire gardens or schoolyards around one theme, such as the "Art Garden" featured on pages 34 to 35. In some garden projects, such as the one at Leeds Elementary School (pages 38 to 39), each grade level has an opportunity to create a plot based on a topic relevant to its curriculum.

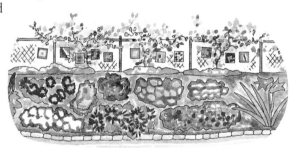

As you and your students consider your teaching and learning goals, think about how a garden designed around a particular theme could help you meet them. For instance, an ethnic or multicultural garden project can prompt students to dig into the cultures represented in the school and local community or those featured in the social studies curriculum. A pollinator garden, in contrast, is a great context for exploring core science concepts such as plant/animal interdependence, honing observation skills, and learning about environmental stewardship.

You might choose a theme that fits with your curriculum goals and have students plan how to bring it to life. Or, consider inviting students to let loose their imaginations and brainstorm ideas and topics *they'd* like for a garden theme. They might even sketch out some of their visions. If you're able to agree on a direction that can also support your learning goals, let the research and planning begin! This section begins with maps and stories that highlight a few schoolyard thematic garden projects. It also features short classroom vignettes, advice, and suggested plants for tackling a host of other themes.

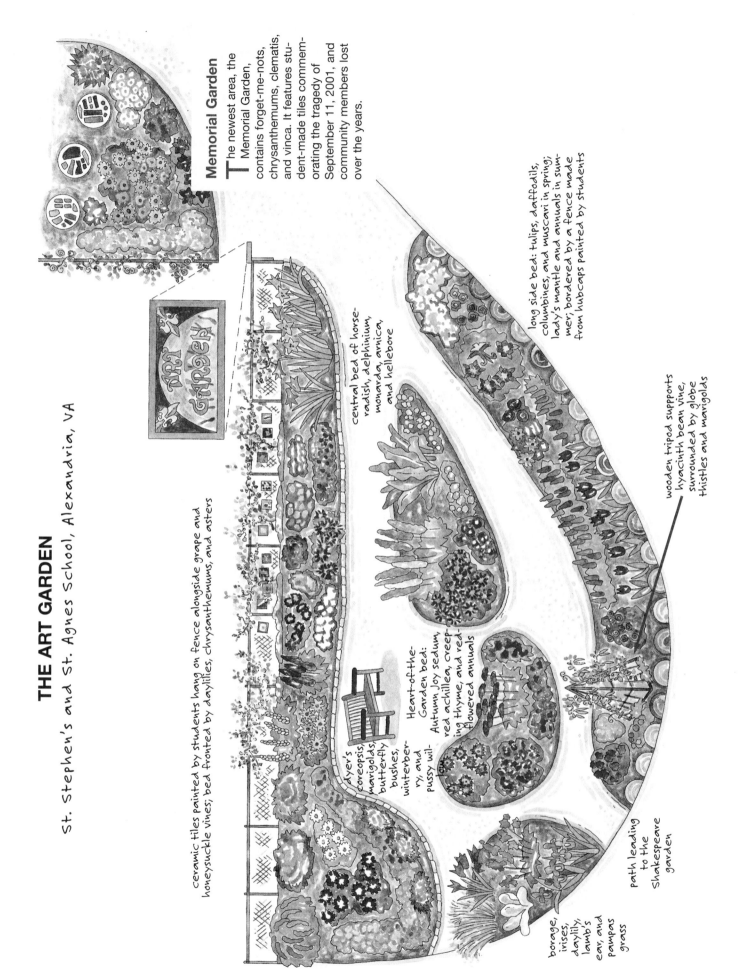

THE ART GARDEN

St. Stephen's and St. Agnes School, Alexandria, VA

Memorial Garden

The newest area, the Memorial Garden, contains forget-me-nots, chrysanthemums, clematis, and vinca. It features student-made tiles commemorating the tragedy of September 11, 2001, and community members lost over the years.

ceramic tiles painted by students hang on fence alongside grape and honeysuckle vines; bed fronted by daylilies, chrysanthemums, and asters

central bed of horse-radish, delphinium, monarda, arnica, and hellebore

long side bed: tulips, daffodils, columbines, and muscari in spring; lady's mantle and annuals in summer; bordered by a fence made from hubcaps painted by students

Tyer's coreopsis, marigolas, butterfly bushes, winterberry, and pussy willow

Heart-of-the-Garden bed: Autumn Joy sedum, red achillea, creeping thyme, and red-flowered annuals

wooden tripod supports hyacinth bean vine, surrounded by globe thistles and marigolds

path leading to the Shakespeare garden

borage, irises, daylily, lamb's ear, and pampas grass

The Art Garden

A Sampling of Art Plants and Projects

Weaving: pampas grass leaves (baskets, mats, wreaths), daylily stems (mats), grapevine and honeysuckle vine (wreaths, baskets)

Paper Making: daylily leaves, iris leaves, pampas grass, and cotton paper pulp (available from *http://toolsforpaper.com*)

Dried Wreath Decorations: grapes, globe thistles, winterberries, hyacinth vine pods

Dyeing: flowers of dyer's coreopsis, marigold, yarrow (magenta), chrysanthemum

Dyeing with Yarrow

Gather leaves and/or flowers and stems anytime from spring to fall. (A dozen plants will sufficiently dye about 4 to 10 ounces of yarn.) Put plants in a large enamel or stainless cooking pot. Cover with water and simmer for one hour. Strain off the golden dyebath. Make sure your cooking area is well ventilated; the odor can be strong.

Add wool or cottton yarn, simmer for one hour, and rinse. (Students can experiment with dye color by adding different amounts of vinegar to the original dye bath.)

(Adapted from A Dyer's Garden, *by Rita Buchanan.)*

Visual arts teacher Kati Towle finds the natural world to be a tempting toolbox. In fact, she envisioned a garden where her middle school students could find plants and flowers for fibers, decorations, and dyes. Once administrators gave the concept a green light and a local Boy Scout troop agreed to clear out construction debris and turn in topsoil, the canvas was set. Now, what was once a 25' x 15' maintenance dump site has been transformed into an oasis of color, art materials, and clever creations.

Kati invited students who signed up for a special summer course to plan the garden, brainstorm ways to use it to support arts education, and begin to design and plant it. After looking at several examples of garden plans, the group explored the types of plants they could use on the basis of their art ideas. Next, they made a chart listing the colors of different flowers so they could plan their palette. Finally, the students walked around the site and discussed planting options and locations.

"Everything we planted that summer had some functional use as an art material," explains Kati. "Certain flowers produced dyes, grasses provided fibers for weaving and making paper, and selected plants could be dried for decoration and fragrance." In subsequent years, as fertile new ideas emerged, the site evolved into a theme garden that incorporates art in many forms. During art classes and recess, youngsters explore color design with plants; paint creative images on benches, hubcaps, tiles, and banners; and use the garden space for activities such as poetry readings and musical performances. They also established the Art Garden Club, which meets weekly throughout the school year.

Fall finds club members planting bulbs and collecting flowers, leaves, and stems to make natural dyes for coloring wool yarn for weaving projects. Each spring, the group creates a decorative work of art, such as mosaic stones or a mural. In the summer art course, students cut foliage from various plants—pampas grass, daylily, and iris—for making handmade "art" paper, and then color the paper pulp with dyes made from yarrow, marigold, and coreopsis (tickseed) flowers.

How They Grew

Kati cautions that this type of project needs a lot of adult support (particularly for summer maintenance), but she also sings its praises. "The students have grown by working together on this project, seeing their ideas come to fruition, learning new ways of making art, and knowing they have created a beautiful space." Proof of their pleasure, she explains, is how much they love hanging out in the garden with friends during recess and after school.

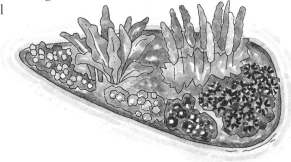

LEXINGTON CREEK BUTTERFLY GARDEN

Lexington Creek Elementary School, Missouri City, TX

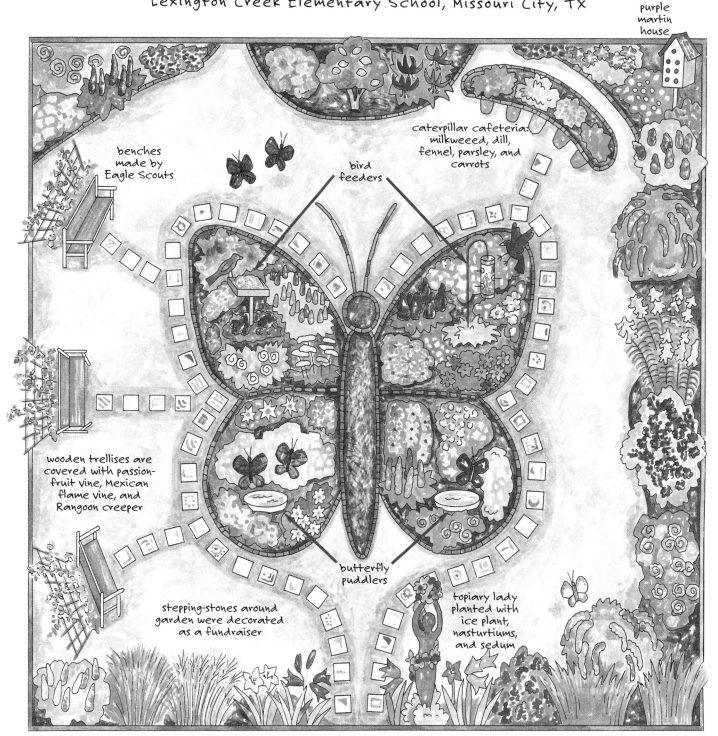

purple martin house

caterpillar cafeteria: milkweeed, dill, fennel, parsley, and carrots

bird feeders

benches made by Eagle Scouts

wooden trellises are covered with passion-fruit vine, Mexican flame vine, and Rangoon creeper

butterfly puddlers

stepping-stones around garden were decorated as a fundraiser

topiary lady planted with ice plant, nasturtiums, and sedum

Food Plants for Butterfly Larvae

Carrot
Dill
Fennel
Milkweed
Native passion vine
Parsley

Community Collaborations Breed Butterflies

Where: *Lexington Creek Elementary School, Missouri City, TX*
Who: *Linda Bartula, butterfly garden chairwoman*

Nectar Plants

For Butterflies
Argentine star grass
Bee balm
Black-eyed Susan
Bluebonnet
Bulbine
Buddleia
Candlestick plant
Caroline aster
Coreopsis
Cosmos
Dianthus
Gaillardia
Gayfeather
Globe amaranth
Lantana
Marigold
Mexican flame vine
Mexican hat
Nasturtium
Penta
Shrimp plant
Sky flower
Sunflower
Tall tails grass
Turk's cap
Verbena
Zinnia

For Hummingbirds
Hamelia
Orange cape
  honeysuckle
Pink cuphae
Rangoon creeper
Russelia
Tecoma stans

The schoolyard at Lexington Creek Elementary spans public land managed by the city park system. Maybe this explains why the entire community got excited over a proposal to establish a 50' x 50' school garden. It began when a volunteer landscape committee of five parents presented a butterfly garden design to the principal, the PTO, and a group of students. "The school is located in an area that has been rapidly transformed from open land to suburban development, resulting in the loss of natural habitat for butterflies," explains former committee Chairwoman Pam Allan. As the idea of creating a habitat took hold, other members of the school and community emerged to offer assistance.

Many Hands Help Project Take Flight
At the garden entrance, a topiary "lady" crafted by the Girl Scouts offers a hearty welcome and reminds visitors how the generosity of an entire community brought the Lexington Creek butterfly garden to life. From there, 100 hand-painted stepping stones guide visitors around the garden. As part of an annual fundraising carnival, families who made donations to the project decorated the stones. It was such a success, organizers offered the activity again the next year, and added shells, glass beads, and colored rocks as potential stone decorations.

Together the landscape committee and students designed the butterfly-shaped flower bed. Master Gardeners shared expertise on water-saving techniques, such as replacing lawn with mulch and incorporating drought-tolerant plants. The local garden club donated money, labor, and plants selected to attract butterflies and hummingbirds, such as purple coneflower. Native plants adapted to the Texas Gulf Coast climate were incorporated wherever possible. The Cub Scouts painted over-turned miniature pots to create plant labels. Boy Scouts spread soil and mulch and constructed bird feeders, birdbaths, and butterfly "puddlers" located in the "wings" of the garden. Special education students fill the puddlers and baths, supplying much-needed water to visiting wildlife.

Visitors can rest on a bench and watch butterflies flit around in search of nectar. Butterfly larvae visit the "caterpillar cafeteria" to feed on milkweed, dill, fennel, parsley, and carrot leaves. A student dreamed up the idea of shaping this bed like a caterpillar with fuzzy "feet" made of dwarf native grasses. Perimeter beds filled with cosmos, pentas, bulbine, and purple fountain grass; wooden trellises supporting Mexican flame vine and Rangoon creeper; and two small ornamental trees attract caterpillars, butterflies, and hummingbirds.

Students and Butterflies Reap the Benefits
In addition to building a sense of community, the butterfly garden prompts 1,000 students at Lexington Creek to explore the natural world. The kindergarten classes hatch and release ladybugs. First graders raise caterpillars in the classroom and release their butterflies onto nectar plants in the spring. Second graders use their vermicompost to enhance garden soil. During a plant science unit, third grade students plant zinnia, gaillardia, and wildflower seeds. Fourth graders monitor the growth and development of the trees they plant on Arbor Day, and fifth graders find artistic inspiration in the garden.

THEMATIC SQUARE-FOOT GARDENS
Leeds Elementary School, Leeds, AL

Cereal Bowl Garden
Features plants that contribute to breakfast cereal ingredients: corn, wheat, rice, sunflowers.

This map shows a blowup of three of the school's square-foot theme gardens. Other plots feature such themes as herbs, five senses, farm crops, pizza, and rainbows. (You can find photos on the school's Web site: *www.leedsel.com*.) Next, the growers hope to create a dinosaur garden featuring plants that were likely around when these giants roamed: ferns, mosses, lycopodiums, hostas, and a ginko tree.

Cloth and Colors Garden
Features plants that have been or are still used to make and dye cloth: cotton and ornamental flax (fiber plants); brown-eyed Susan, false indigo, calendula (dye plants).

Old World/New World
Features plants that originated on this continent and those that were brought here by explorers and immigrants. **Old World:** beets, broccoli, carrots, lettuce, onions. **New World:** beans, peppers, tomatoes, strawberries (squash grown in larger plot).

Thematic Square-Foot Gardens

Where: *Leeds Elementary School, Leeds, AL*
Who: *Shirley Farrell, teacher of gifted and schoolwide enrichment*

Square-Foot Gardens

A square-foot garden typically consists of a 3'x 3' (or 2'x 2') raised bed filled with rich soil, or a moveable box filled with equal parts compost, peat moss, and vermiculite. Each square foot in the grid can be used to grow a different crop, with the number of plants per square varying with individual plant space needs. If you have minimal school gardening space, or simply want to start small, consider using this system.

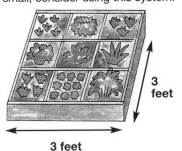

3 feet

3 feet

Shirley Farrell knew that if teachers are excited about a project, kids will be too. And she knew her colleagues would be more enthusiastic if the project truly supported the curriculum. Her own students had already delved into gardening, so when an Eagle Scout offered to build 15 raised beds measuring 3'x 3'x 1' high, she seized the opportunity to engage the school in a square-foot-gardening adventure.

Tackling Design

Interested teachers got together to brainstorm themes that could help them address learning goals in different areas, and then presented their thoughts for their classes to consider. Students added their own ideas to the lists, and each class voted on a theme for its unique 9-square-foot plot. The youngsters first had to figure out which plants their gardens should contain and how tall each might grow. Students sketched designs to scale on graph paper and each class either voted on one or combined ideas in a new design. "During the planning and planting phase, math concepts with which students had previously struggled—measurement, perimeter, area—came to life," says Shirley. "Younger students, for instance, stapled 12-inch straws along the edges, and then connected straws across the width of the bed to create each of the 9 square feet."

"As the number of gardens and our outdoor classroom areas grew, I realized I needed more help, so I created an intensive gardening course called Junior Garden Leaders for my gifted fourth and fifth graders," explains Shirley. These kids lend support to other classes as they plant and tend their gardens.

Digging into Themes

Shirley explains that each teacher had a unique strategy for engaging students with the class's chosen theme. The "Cereal Bowl Garden" emerged when first graders tried to find pictures of plants on the cereal boxes they had brought in. After reading the ingredient lists as a class, they identified even more plants: corn, wheat, rice, sunflower oil, and so on. A local farm store donated many of those seeds, which the kids promptly planted. "Some of the kids were amazed to see grass growing where we had planted our seeds, and they wanted to pull it up," explains Shirley. That prompted a discussion about how vital grasses are to our nutrition.

For the "Old World/New World Garden," fourth graders were challenged to choose a vegetable garden plant or farm crop and then dig into its past: its origin and uses, and how it came to this country. Research via books, the Internet, and seed catalogs yielded lively visual presentations and intriguing information. "The kids were amazed to discover that tomatoes were once considered poisonous, that potatoes were assumed to be unfit for human consumption, and that many of our favorite food plants came from our own country," says Shirley.

The compact square-foot gardens turned out to be very manageable for teachers and students, Shirley reports. Once they had gotten comfortable growing things, several classes were inspired to expand to larger-sized plots to create a Three Sisters Native American planting system, a hummingbird garden, and more. "Most students don't really think of plants as living things, nor do they appreciate plants' diversity, histories, and range of purposes," says Shirley. "Their focus on selected themes sparked their interest in learning more. It's not uncommon now to hear, 'Hey, this shirt has cotton,' or 'I found corn in this new cereal.'"

CHILDREN'S HISTORY GARDEN
Paul H. Cale Elementary School, Charlottesville, VA

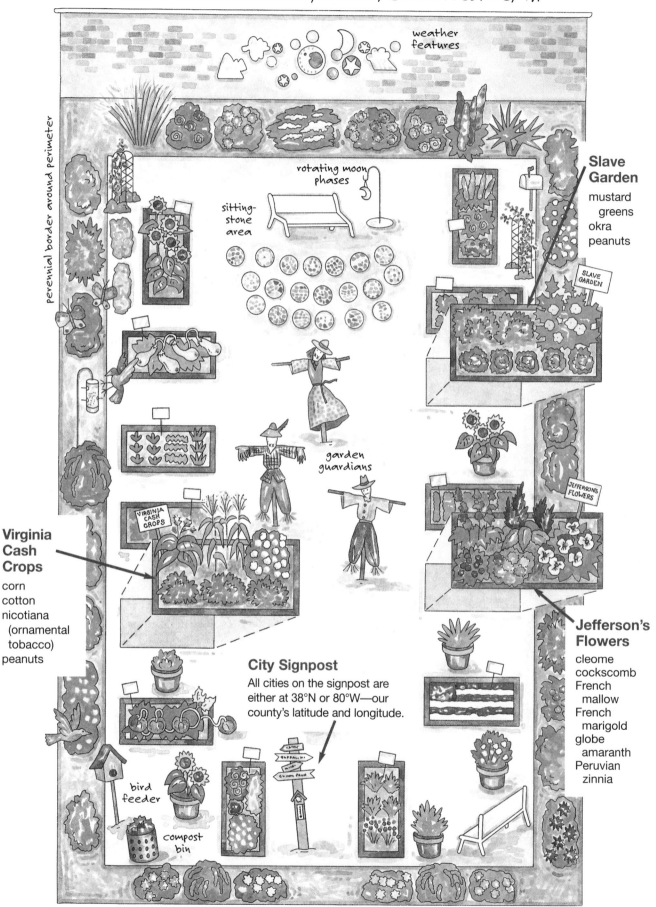

weather features

rotating moon phases

sitting-stone area

perennial border around perimeter

garden guardians

Slave Garden

mustard greens
okra
peanuts

SLAVE GARDEN

JEFFERSON'S FLOWERS

Virginia Cash Crops

corn
cotton
nicotiana
(ornamental tobacco)
peanuts

VIRGINIA CASH CROPS

Jefferson's Flowers

cleome
cockscomb
French mallow
French marigold
globe amaranth
Peruvian zinnia

City Signpost

All cities on the signpost are either at 38°N or 80°W—our county's latitude and longitude.

bird feeder

compost bin

Children's History Garden

Where: *Paul H. Cale Elementary School, Charlottesville, VA*
Who: *Phyllis Davidson, teacher*

Recommended Resources

- Thomas Jefferson Center's Twinleaf catalog. Features seed samplers for historic plants: *http://shop.store.yahoo.com/twinleafcatalogue/seed-samplers.html*

- American Slave Gardens. An overview of garden styles and vegetables: *www.northbysouth.org/1999/food/neh/gardens.htm*

- Agriculture in the Classroom. Search for your state's contact information on this national Web site. Each state has a wealth of educational resources: *www.agclassroom.org*

Students' laminated garden sign

Phyllis Davidson's fourth graders needed to study Virginia history, but, she explains, social studies simply seemed dead to many of them. Her solution was to create a school garden that would help bring the state's rich history to life, establish a sense of place, and integrate science and art objectives.

Before digging into the past, Phyllis's youngsters laid out the 75' x 40' site. "First, we created a border featuring perennial flowers and shrubs," says Phyllis. The class chose some plants, such as liatris, to attract butterflies, and others, such as lemon thyme, for their scintillating aromas. Each year, they add annuals, such as poppies, for the colorful surprises they offer. Inside this border, the students created 13 2m x 1m beds with brick perimeters, temporarily marking each one with a 5" x 7" metal sign displaying the name of one of the 13 original colonies. Once students in each grade had a chance to plan and plant one of these beds with a unique theme, they'd replace the sign with a descriptive laminated one.

The fourth graders, focused on planting the past, devoted three beds on aspects of the state's history. Here's what they created:

Virginia Historic Cash Crops Garden. The fourth grade curriculum requires students to explore agriculture's influence on the colony and the institution of slavery. "We discovered that when the London Company started Jamestown to make money, they discovered that tobacco, cotton, corn, and peanuts could be big sellers," explains Phyllis. She adds that the theme garden that bears these crops—each fascinating in its own right—has inspired a host of pithy discussions: *How could tobacco have saved Virginia financially, but then killed so many citizens? Why didn't they have many slaves in the North?*

Slave Garden. Student investigations turned up plants that were common to slaves' gardens and tables. These included some that were native to Africa, such as okra and leafy greens. The young sleuths discovered that other plants, such as peanuts, originated in South America, were taken back to Europe by Spanish explorers, and then spread to Asia and Africa via traders. When Africans were forced to come here as slaves, many carried peanut seeds with them.

Jefferson's Flowers. "Our study of Thomas Jefferson revealed that he was a man of wide interests: a scientist, a plantation owner, and a gardener," explains Phyllis. She obtained packets of seeds representing Jefferson's favorite flowers from the Thomas Jefferson Center for Historic Plants, and another two garden plots took shape.

More Angles on History

"As we selected plants for other parts of our garden, we always looked for opportunities to connect to history," says Phyllis. For instance, each of the flower-filled terra-cotta containers scattered throughout the site has a laminated sign with the name of a historical person such as explorer Meriweather Lewis, Pocahontas, and the first four presidents from Virginia. The garden's perennial border features a flower with a Latin name (*Clarkia pulchella*) that honors its "discoverer." (Lewis and Clark brought it back from their Northwest explorations.) The original ship that landed in Jamestown and other images from the past are depicted on the student-designed mosaic sitting stones.

Short Takes on Themes

We hope the stories and descriptions of theme gardens in the next 10 pages spark your thinking about even more projects and designs. These examples represent a just fraction of the themes now taking form in school gardens nationwide. Your *best* source of ideas might well be your students' fertile young minds.

The Three Sisters: Native American Gardening

Although native peoples from different parts of North America used a wide range of agricultural techniques, perhaps the best-known one is the interplanting of corn, beans, and squash: a trio called by many groups "The Three Sisters." Numerous school gardeners in our network have experimented with Three Sisters and other Native American plantings, and others have expressed interest in doing so.

This well-conceived planting system features three crops that benefit one another and together nourish the people who plant them. The corn supports the bean vines as they grow upward, and the squash covers the soil, helping control weeds and deter predators who might feed on the corn. The beans can convert nitrogen from the air into a form that plants can use. (The nitrogen remaining after the beans have grown will be available for the corn, which requires a good deal of the nutrient, the following year.) The sisters also complement each other nutritionally, with the corn supplying carbohydrates, beans contributing protein and additional vitamins, and squash offering lots of vitamin A.

It's hardly surprising that these crops—considered by many to be special gifts from the creator—played such an important role in the agriculture and nutrition of most of the native peoples of the Americas. Because of the Sisters' central role as "sustainers of life," a host of stories, customs, celebrations, and ceremonies are associated with them.

Each native culture that grew the Three Sisters had a unique planting system. Here we feature guidelines for a design often used in the Northeast.

Select and Prepare a Site

You'll want to plant your Three Sisters Garden in late spring once the danger of frost has passed. Choose a site that has direct sunshine for most of the day and access to water. Once students have determined their site's dimensions, challenge them to plan their Three Sisters Garden on paper. They can use the layout suggested on the next page or research others and try them out.

First, break up and rake the soil. Next, build a mound about 12 inches high and between 18 inches and 3 feet in diameter. If you're in a dry area, flatten the top of the mound and make a shallow depression to keep water from running off. The number of mounds your students create depends on the size of your growing area. Mounds should be 3 to 4 feet apart in all directions.

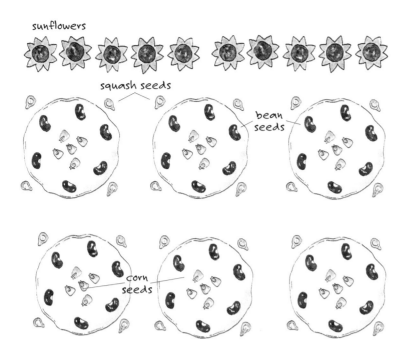

sunflowers

squash seeds

bean seeds

corn seeds

Make corn, bean, and squash mounds 3' to 4' apart.

Plant the Site

Corn. Soak four to seven corn seeds per mound overnight and then plant them about 6 inches apart in the center of each mound. (You'll eventually thin to three or four seedlings.) Many native people honor the tradition of giving thanks to the "Four Directions" by orienting the corn seeds to the north, south, east, and west. By doing the same, students can learn to use compasses and observe the sun's movements.

Beans and squash. After a week or two, when the corn is at least 4 inches high, soak and then plant six pole bean seeds in a circle about 6 inches away from the corn. (You'll eventually thin to three or four bean seedlings.) At about the same time, plant four squash or pumpkin seeds next to the mound, about a foot away from the beans, eventually thinning to one. If you are planting a large area, you can also sow the squash in separate mounds (1 foot in diameter) near every few corn and bean mounds.

Consider Other Additions

Consider planting other traditional crops, such as sunflowers or jerusalem artichokes (a tuberous perennial sunflower), around the Three Sisters Garden. Put these tall crops on the north side so they won't shade your other plants. Potatoes, sweet potatoes, and other native crops are often planted in nearby plots. Some of the many other indigenous plants used by native North, South, and Central Americans include melons, tobacco, chili peppers, cotton, blueberries, wild rice, and hazelnuts. Your students might let their creative juices flow as they create a unique scarecrow. A number of native cultures' gardens incorporate these familiar figures.

Help the Three Sisters Grow Stronger

As corn plants grow, weed gently around them and mound soil at the base of each stem for support. When the corn is knee-high and again when silks appear on the husks, it helps to "side-dress" by putting a high-nitrogen fertilizer (such as aged manure or fish emulsion) on the soil surface near each plant. If beans aren't winding their way around the corn, youngsters can help by moving tendrils to the stalks. (Keen observers may notice a pattern in the direction in which the bean vines wind.) To allow room for corn and beans to grow, gently direct squash vines into walkways, garden edges, or between mounds. Once students observe young fruits, side-dress the squash plants with aged manure or compost. If you pinch off the tips of squash runners after several fruits have started to form, the plants will devote more energy to producing squash.

Where: *Cameron Middle School, Nashville, TN*
Who: *Sue Luchs, teacher*

Historic Herb Gardens

"As a middle school science and social studies teacher, I've always been interested in helping students appreciate the impact of food on history," reports Nashville, TN, teacher Sue Luchs. "When I had a chance to manage our school herb garden, it made sense to use a historical lens."

The living history garden the students researched and created represented five regions and eras. Here's an overview of a few of their gardens:

Ancient and Medieval Europe. Here, students come to appreciate the importance of herbs during this era for masking odors and flavors associated with such factors as food spoilage, tooth decay, and limited hygiene. Mints and pest repellents such as pennyroyal, tansy, and wormwood are garden staples. Other featured herbs include chamomile, lavender, and rosemary, which were traditionally strewn on floors to cover odors and repel pests. Students used plants from this garden to create potpourri and cook medieval feasts.

Middle East and Africa. This planting features early Egyptian dye plants, such as dyer's broom and henna, and fiber plants such as flax, which were used to make clothing. Students harvested mint from this garden to create a salve to use on burns and cuts.

Western Hemisphere. This garden includes plants native to the Americas as well as those introduced by European settlers. Students explore how herbs were used by Native Americans, colonists, and soldiers in the Civil War. The class made "bandages," for instance, from mullein leaves dipped into hot water and then into a bowl of cool vinegar. Another highlight was steeping homegrown Oswego tea (bee balm) after discovering that the Oswego Indians gave this to colonists to replace their English tea discarded during the famous Tea Party.

"This project brought the past to life, and also enabled my many non-native English speakers to share their knowledge about plants from their own cultures," explains Sue.

Native Intelligence: Students Revive a Prairie

Wildflowers in a can would be the *last* thing a group of fourth graders in Clinton, WI, would plant in their schoolyard. They've set their sights on the return of the natives, the tallgrass prairies that, says teacher Kim Lowman Vollmer, are more endangered than the rainforest.

Inspired by Rachel Carson's model of taking action to make a difference in the environment, Kim and her fourth graders turned a barren 40' x 120' area into a native prairie. Before putting trowels to soil, each student chose a native prairie plant, then learned what its history was, how it was used by Native Americans and European pioneers, and how it supports wildlife. He or she created a class presentation combining this research with catalog pictures and information on the plant's size, color, and bloom times.

Soliciting Donations

To tackle their prairie project vision, Kim's class realized they would need to get others to invest in the outcome. So, using Kid Pix software, students created a computer slide show with pictures, graphics, and narration to share with other classes, the school board, and potential supporters. And they reaped heaps. A community foundation grant yielded funds, local businesses donated services and materials (such as wood chips), high school students helped spread and level sand, and middle schoolers built specially designed Aldo Leopold benches. Meanwhile, Kim's students held a successful "pennies for prairies" fundraiser.

Digging In

To accomplish the task of putting in 3,000 plants representing 65 species, the class divided the area into smaller patches. Pairs of youngsters then worked in an area to measure where each grass or forb (non-grass prairie plant) should be placed. "The kids were particularly careful placing the four types of plants that are on the state's endangered species

Why Go Native?

One way of preserving habitat health in schoolyard projects is to try to plant or maintain as many native plants as possible. A plant that is considered native to an area has evolved in a region over time and developed complex, interdependent relationships with other organisms.

Native plants are better designed to meet regional wildlife needs and, because they have adapted to local climatic conditions and soils, they are typically easy to maintain. Always try to obtain native plants from local or regional sources, or start your own from collected seeds of plants that are plentiful. Never dig up wild plants unless you're rescuing them from a spot where they are in danger of being destroyed, such as a construction site.

list," explains Kim. Once the area was laid out, her students invited younger kids to help with the massive planting effort.

Curriculum goals were front and center as students traced how the land was used historically, created prairie-inspired art projects, kept detailed journals of the habitat's development, and observed and compared its plants and organisms. "The prairie quickly became home to butterflies, toads, birds, bees, and even a rare great golden digger wasp," says Kim. "It also provided the impetus for students' becoming 'phenologists,'" she adds. (Phenologists are those who track seasonal weather-influenced changes in plants and animals.) Her pupils routinely predict "firsts" (blooms, appearance of birds, and so on), and try to link them to local weather and broader climatic conditions.

How They Grew

The pride Kim's students feel in having created this sanctuary for plants, wildlife, and people has become apparent, she says, as they give tours to other classes and community members. "I've seen them invite younger children to smell mints, show them how a cup plant actually holds water, and explain why it's important to care for endangered plants and the wildlife that depends on them," says Kim. "You know, anything, no matter how small, can make a difference. Children need chances to be involved and interested in their outdoor world and to learn what it means to become good stewards of the environment."

Note: Many organizations located throughout much of the middle region of the country are concerned about the loss of native prairies. Many of these groups assist schools with prairie restoration or simulation projects. To find out if any such resources or projects exist in your area, contact your regional botanic gardens, Natural Resources Conservation Service, or similar agencies.

Ethnic Gardens (Cultivating Cross-Culturally)

"Since foods can be a window on cultural understanding and appreciation, we're attempting to open that window with an after-school kids' garden for 'at-risk' youngsters that features foods of ethnic groups who live in our city," reports Master Gardener Vernon Mullens. The project has borrowed the African word *sankofa*, which means "Go back and fetch it," since youngsters gather cultural information and, through plants, explore current and historical aspects of the groups that make up their community.

In addition to learning to raise, care for, and harvest a garden, students research the origins and histories of the foods they're growing, locate on maps where crops originated and where they're used today, and learn about their nutritional value. "The kids particularly enjoy asking parents and seniors how they've used different crops, trying new foods, and bringing new ethnic recipes home," Vernon notes.

Here's an overview of plants found in three of the project's ethnic gardens.

Asian Garden: soybeans, Chinese cabbage and other greens, lettuce, radishes, cucumbers, spinach, ginger, eggplants.

Central American Garden: corn, winter squash, potatoes, chili peppers, pumpkins, beans, tithonia (Mexican sunflower).

African-American Garden: collards, mustard and turnip greens, broadbeans, ginger, hot peppers, peanuts, watermelon, okra, sweet potatoes, and basil. They represent crops brought from Africa and crops native to this country that African-Americans cultivated and used.

Rainbow Garden

Where: *Parkview Elementary School, San Jose, CA*
Who: *Tina Margason, teacher*

"A garden is a place where kids' imaginations thrive and everything is a miracle," observes San Jose, CA, teacher Tina Margason. "Wouldn't it be fun if we could plant our own rainbow?" her students asked after reading Lois Ehlert's *Planting a Rainbow*. To launch the project, the class scavenged a wide variety of flower seed packets and sorted them by color. They used seed catalogs to find more flowers to fill in the gaps. Using the rainbow book as a model for the color scheme, students planned the garden, assigning multiple types of flowers to each hue. "The kids had to solve problems along the way," explains Tina. "Sometimes it was tough to decide whether a particular flower belonged in the red or violet band, for instance." Students planted seeds indoors in carefully marked pots, then transplanted them to the garden in the spring.

Although not all of the daffodils, amaryllis, zinnias, marigolds, black-eyed Susans, alyssum, and other flowers bloomed at once, reports Tina, students were thrilled each time a new color appeared. Their journals depicted each new event and emergence, and predicted how the rainbow would change over time. "When the kids returned in the fall, their rainbow gardens had evolved with a new range of hues," reports Tina. "They came to appreciate that 'miracles' indeed take patience."

A Rainbow of Easy Annuals	
COLOR	PLANT
Green	'Envy' zinnia
	bells of Ireland
	lettuce
Blue	ageratum
	nierembergia
	salvia
	cornflower
	lobelia
Purple	petunia
	verbena
Pink	snapdragon
	cleome
	petunia
	nicotiana
	cosmos
	zinnia
Red	scarlet salvia
	zinnia
	snapdragon
Orange	marigold
	zinnia
	cosmos
	tithonia
Yellow	gloriosa daisy
	snapdragon
	zinnia
	marigold
White	nicotiana
	petunia
	cosmos
	cleome
	sweet alyssum

Planting Tips for a Blooming Rainbow

You can grow a blooming rainbow by planting curved rows of different-colored flowers. For the best effect, use plants that have similar heights. The sidebar (right) has suggestions for easy annuals to make up the rainbow.

Bird-Friendly Garden

Where: *South Cache Freshman Center, Hyrum, UT*
Who: *Ron Helstern, teacher*

"When my ninth graders decided to increase the diversity of life on our school site, they were particularly interested in attracting birds, since we were participating in Cornell's Project FeederWatch," reports Hyrum, UT, teacher Ron Helstern. When they first inventoried their site, students found no live birds—just one dead Western meadowlark. To learn more about bird habitat needs, the class set up research teams and visited a local Audubon center. Each student next inventoried a 3m x 3m plot to determine what plants grew naturally on the school site. "Because the plots were so big, I had students identify and count plants in square-meter sections, then estimate the number of each plant species in the full plot," says Paul. With a better understanding of what the site

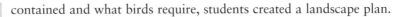

contained and what birds require, students created a landscape plan.

Next, they approached nurseries and discount stores for late-season plant donations, saved seeds from annuals and perennials to grow in the classroom, and secured EPA grant funds to purchase trees, feeders, and other features. Choke-cherries, apricots, honeysuckle, wild roses, sunflowers, and raspberries are some of the species the bird-friendly site now boasts. "It's amazing to see teenagers, who typically think the universe revolves around them, so inspired by the dozens of bird species (and other forms of wildlife) that visit our site," says Paul. "They love being able to identify them by sight and sound, and are genuinely eager to learn more about the habitat problems these creatures face," he adds.

Hosting Feathered Friends

Like other animals, birds need food, water, shelter, and safe places to rear their young. A diversity of plant types—trees, shrubs, perennials, grasses, and so on—can help feed, shelter, and protect a wide range of avian visitors. Seed-eaters, such as goldfinches, like sunflowers and sun-loving perennials: purple coneflower, black-eyed Susan, and thistle. Hummingbirds thrive on bright nectar-producing flowers: aloe, bee balm, butterfly bush, columbine, cardinal flower, honeysuckle, and sage. Shrubs and trees with berries, fruits, nuts, or sap, such as Russian olive, raspberry, blueberry, pecan, and oak, are another key food source. Be sure to include some plants, like highbush cranberry, that hold on to their fruits through the winter. And grasses and legumes left unmowed can provide seeds and cover for ground nesters.

Pollinator Garden

Butterfly gardens, such as the one described on pages 36 to 37 are a favorite and enticing schoolyard theme. But these winged beauties, who help move pollen from male to female flowers so fertilization and seed production can occur, are *hardly* the only such partners. In fact, thousands of different animal species help pollinate plants, including bees of all sizes, tiny wasps, moths, flies, bats, and hummingbirds.

By creating a garden that attracts a variety of pollinators, students can provide vital oases amidst deserts of buildings and concrete. They can, in turn, use these living laboratories to explore plants, animal visitors, and the ways in which the threads of life connect. Don't feel limited by your available space. Even a small container planting can entice and feed pollinators. Here are some guidelines for cultivating gardens that appeal to these important plant partners.

Plant plenty of nectar- and pollen-rich flowers. Use as many native plants as possible, since local plants and pollinators are more likely to be adapted to one another. Also shoot for old-fashioned varieties. Although hybrid flowers are bred to look or smell nice for humans, they often don't provide much accessible nectar or pollen for animal partners.

Include a variety of flowers that bloom throughout the season. By doing so, you will accommodate different pollinators' preferences and provide a sequence of pollen and nectar sources throughout different stages of the life cycle.

Try to get flowers with a range of shapes and sizes. Trumpet or cup-shaped flowers, such as cardinal flower, honeysuckle, and bee balm, attract a wide range of pollinators. Pollinators with shorter tongues, such as small native bees and wasps, feed on tightly packed clusters of small flowers, such as those found on milkweed, zinnia, phlox, and mint. Hummingbirds feed

Pollinator-Friendly Plants

PLANT	POLLINATOR
zinnia	bees, wasps
phlox	bees, wasps
mint	bees, wasps
rose	beetles
magnolia	beetles
butterfly bush	butterflies
calendula	butterflies
zinnia	butterflies
bleeding heart	hummingbirds
fuschia	hummingbirds
sage	hummingbirds
nasturtium	hummingbirds
evening primrose	moths
yucca	moths
flowering tobacco	moths
cardinal flower	many
honeysuckle	many
bee balm	many
milkweed	many

on red, purple, or orange flowers with lots of nectar, such as bee balm, fuschia, sage, and nasturtium.

Provide food sources (host plants) and overwintering places for eggs and larvae. Allow a section of your schoolyard to revert to wild grasses, weeds, and wildflowers (e.g., milkweed and Queen Anne's lace) and plant dill and parsley for larvae.

Provide water. Pollinators such as butterflies can gather and sip at shallow pools, mud puddles, and birdbaths, and bees and wasps can use mud as a home-building material.

Avoid using pesticides and herbicides. Many can be harmful to pollinators as well as pests. Herbicides may wipe out key plants (weeds) that are important for pollinators' food mix. If you feel that you must control pests, judiciously use homemade remedies such as garlic spray, or pesticides derived from plants or microbes. Apply them only after sundown, when most pollinators have stopped their rounds.

Provide nesting sites and materials. Leave cut plant stems exposed, turn flowerpots with bottom holes upside down, leave twigs and brush in small piles, create mud puddles, or put out pieces of string or other light fibers.

Storybook Garden

"My third graders were reading a story about aliens who were doing science experiments with vegetables, and we got to talking about other books that featured plants," says teacher Jean Sasabuchi. After all, green living things were their science focus that year. The youngsters first brainstormed books that featured plants or plant foods, and then went to the library in search of those and more. "The kids were amazed at the volume of plant-based books, so I had each one choose a book and then identify a few plants he or she would like to grow in our garden," says Jean. Students first copied their selected book covers, and then laminated them and staked them in a small garden square. "The kids kept track of plant growth and introduced younger buddies to their storybook plots," says Jean. "Reading also became much more exciting because students were motivated to look for plant words and growing ideas in whatever they came across."

What books can inspire storybook plantings?

Where: *Cooper School, Vacaville, CA*
Who: *Jean Sasabuchi, teacher*

Alphabet Garden

Learning the alphabet takes on new meaning when it's thriving and blooming. Seed packets, catalogs, and gardening books can fuel the search for plants starting with different letters. Your students will have an easier time if they consider the Latin name as well as the familiy and common names for plants in their search, and be flexible. For example, they might decide that Queen Anne's lace could be used for *Q, A,* or *L.* If a suitable plant is unavailable or impractical, students might decide to include a letter via a sign or an interesting object that begins with that letter. The letter *X* is tough, but the lovely dried flower immortelle is a good choice. Its Latin name is *xeranthemum.*

Where: *Beaty Warren Middle School, Warren, PA*
Who: *Mark Davis, teacher*

Here a few ideas to get you started:

Allison's Zinnia	*Peter Rabbit*
Anna's Garden Songs	*Seedfolks*
City Green	*Tops and Bottoms*
The Giant Turnip	*The Maybe Garden*
Growing Vegetable Soup	*The Little Red Hen*
Linnea in Monet's Garden	*Where the Lilies Bloom*
Miss Rumphius	*Wise Child*

Besides raising plants that appear in stories, students can take the storybook theme farther: they can create story characters from natural materials or painted plywood cutouts; add whimsical details, such as twig furniture, fences, or Peter Rabbit's blue jacket; and create sitting areas for enjoying stories.

Historical Garden of Peace and Healing

"A few years ago one of my students was harassed by other kids for reading a book about an African-American," reports Warren, PA, middle school teacher Mark Davis.

"When I shared this with my ecology club students, they wondered what they could do to inspire students in our homogeneous school to appreciate and respect human diversity and develop better skills for handling problems," he says. The outcome of their musings? A vision of a "garden of healing" for the school and community.

A catalog from the American Forests' Famous and Historical Trees program pushed students' thinking further. It offers tree seedlings associated with significant events and people in American history—peacemakers, freedom fighters, and inventors, for instance. The ecology club's first initiative was to honor George Washington Carver by buying and planting a green ash seedling descended from a tree on his laboratory site. "The girls in the club immediately requested that we also acknowledge inspiring women," reports Mark. "So we raised more funds to purchase a red bud tree related to one of Clara Barton's and a sycamore linked to Susan B. Anthony."

During the next few years, the concept—and the trees— flourished. With support from a local foundation grant, the healing garden evolved into five areas to represent good citizenship and the events and people who have modeled its virtues. These areas include the Circle of Caring, Circle of Hope, Walk of New Ideas and Service, and Walk of Courage. Each section honors people of high ideals and committed service to fellow humans. The emerging Trail of Peace honors Nobel Peace Prize winners, the Iroquois Peace Confederacy, and those who walked the Trail of Tears. So far it features a sycamore honoring Martin Luther King and white pines representing the Iroquois Federation.

Student-made signs in each section invite those who visit to reflect on the virtues symbolized by the plantings. For instance, one sign reads, *May all who walk this trail work toward living in harmony.* "Since students also wanted appropriate plants that would offer more immediate beauty, we created a literal garden of healing by planting native flowers that early Americans believed induced health," says Mark. This included sunflowers (used to make a tea and salve for a range of ailments), butterfly weed (used for lung inflammations), and bee balm (used as a tea for stomachaches, colds, and insomnia).

"The garden has given these adolescents some concrete ways to focus their minds and energy and to consider the virtues that are vital to a healthy community," notes Mark. "It has also enabled students and community members to become aware of what historical figures (including minorities) have done to help our country grow and heal. Last year, the incoming fourth graders, who had heard about our garden, made peace cranes and brought flowers to plant when they visited. In a very powerful ceremony, we burned the peace cranes and put the ashes on the flowers in the Trail of Peace," he explains.

American Forests offers a variety of seedlings of famous and historic trees along with a wealth of historic information in its catalog. Call (800) 320-8733 for a copy.

Theme Garden Snapshots

Here are some more inspiring ideas we've gleaned from schoolyards throughout the country.

Science Concepts

You might design a plot for exploring specific science concepts or ideas, such as adaptations. With that theme as a backdrop, you could grow flowers with dramatic adaptations for pollination (bright designs, large stamens, and so on), plants that "do things," such as mimosas (which close their leaves when they're touched); or plants with tendrils for climbing, such as beans.

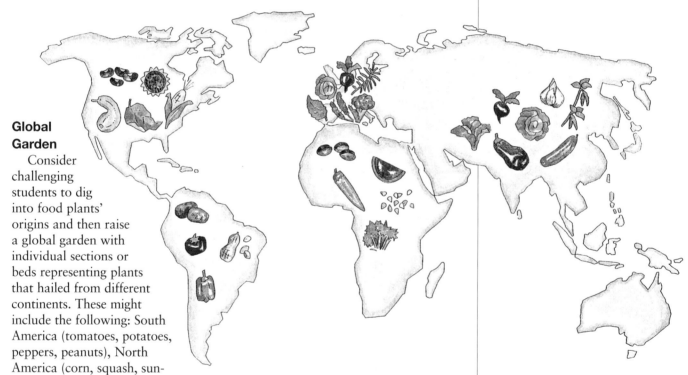

Global Garden

Consider challenging students to dig into food plants' origins and then raise a global garden with individual sections or beds representing plants that hailed from different continents. These might include the following: South America (tomatoes, potatoes, peppers, peanuts), North America (corn, squash, sunflowers, beans, tobacco), Europe (lavender, peppermint, rosemary, beets, broccoli, cabbages, turnips), Africa (watermelons, sesame, coffee, okra, parsley), and Asia (soybeans, radishes, eggplants, cucumbers, garlic, spinach, lettuce).

Peace Pole Garden

The international Peace Pole Project promotes world peace by asking people to "plant" an 8-foot-tall pole made of hardwood, plastic, or metal, and to write the message *May Peace Prevail on Earth* on each of its four or six sides. (Ideally, the message is written in different languages.) These monuments announce that this is a special place dedicated to peace on Earth, and they serve as a focal point for gatherings and ceremonies. In some schoolyards, Peace Poles are surrounded by gardens. At Barnett Shoals School in Athens, GA, the plants bloom in school colors.

Culinary Herbs

Students in Leeds, AL, surveyed families to learn about favorite herbs and spices, and then filled each square foot with an herb: globe basil, purple basil, lemon grass, cilantro, dill, thyme, rosemary, peppermint, parsley, and chive.

Cool Container Garden

If recycling is something you want your students to value, consider asking them to come up with novel planting containers that would otherwise have been trash. At Flor del Sol School in Phoenix, AZ, students have tomatoes and houseplants sprouting in old wheelbarrows and in old shoes and boots they've painted. A stack of painted tires hosts potatoes. Meanwhile, at Buchanan Middle School in Michigan, an old rural mailbox, a lantern, and other recycled containers sport living flower bouquets.

Pizza Garden

If your students create a circular pizza garden, they can shape beds like pie slices with paths in between. Tomatoes, peppers, onions, oregano, garlic, parsley, and basil complete the picture—and lead the way to a pizza party.

Sensory (Sense-Sational) Garden

Many schoolyards display gardens with plants that both stimulate and soothe the senses. Plants kids like to touch include fuzzy lamb's ear and wooly thyme, prickly coneflowers and strawflowers, and touch-me-not pods (which spurt out seeds). Making the "faces" of snapdragon flowers talk (while learning a bit about how they're pollinated) is also popular. Scented geraniums, sweet peas, heliotropes, Oriental lilies, and a host of herbs provide aromatic interest. Kids like to taste plants such as dill, chocolate mint, nasturtium, and violets. Bright colors are visually stimulating, but so are surprising ones, such as purple carrots, and extremes of size, such as huge sunflowers and tiny tomatoes.

Farm Garden

By researching and planting a garden of farm crops grown in your region, or in the U.S., students can delve into where food comes from and what happens to it on its way to their tables. The farm garden at Leeds Elementary School (page 38) features contemporary local farm crops such as cotton, peanuts, wheat, oats, soybeans, and sweet potatoes, as well as old crops such as broom corn. Fifth graders study the history of the U.S., including the farm crops once grown, and those still grown, in the South. After they harvest the crops, they separate the cotton fibers from the seeds, grind wheat into flour, shell beans, and make brooms from broom corn.

Sundial Garden

We've spoken with some students who are researching plants, such as four o'clocks, that bloom at certain times of day.

Tea Time Garden

Your students might grow herbal teas to steep and taste test or to dry, package, and sell. German chamomile, calendula, lemon verbena, peppermint, bronze fennel, lemongrass, and lemon balm are good candidates.

Students Create Smokin' Dragon Garden

Chicago Botanic Garden's Rory Klick recalls a brainstorming session she participated in with a second grade class. When one boy suggested the class create a "dragon" theme garden, Rory challenged him to consider what they would plant in such a garden. He quickly responded, "snapdragons, of course." (He liked the way snapdragon flowers opened their "mouths.") Well-versed in taking advantage of "teachable moments," she asked the class to research other plants that would fit the dragon theme. With help from their teacher and a parent, students identified a list of plants to include in what they dubbed their "Smokin' Dragon Garden Zone." In their designated garden plot, the second graders complemented their snapdragons with smokebush (*Cotinus coggygria*), burning bush (*Euonymus alata* 'Compacta'), fireweed (*Epilobium angustifolium*), and red hot poker (*Kniphofia tritoma*). To complete the theme, they painted a concrete alligator to resemble a dragon and placed it among the snapdragons. A vibrant, student-created sign welcomed visitors to the garden and helped explain the theme.

Resources

Web Sites

4-H Children's Garden at Michigan State University
http://4hgarden.msu.edu/tour/overview.html

Take a virtual tour of the children's garden that has been hailed as "the most creative half-acre in America." Click on a map of the garden to zoom in on any one of the 56 individual theme gardens.

Boston Schoolyard Initiative
www.schoolyards.org

This Web site presents a model for schoolyard transformation. It highlights the process the Boston Schoolyard Initiative developed to create schoolyard oases in its own region. It covers topics such as developing partnerships, community collaboration, the participatory design process, sustainability, and curriculum connections.

The Edible Schoolyard
www.edibleschoolyard.org

Here, you can read about the now-famous transformation of an abandoned lot adjacent to the Martin Luther King Jr. Middle School in Berkeley, CA. The project offers a compelling model for transforming the way children feel about education, food, and the Earth.

Evergreen
www.evergreen.ca/en/lg/lg.html

From this Canadian environmental education organization's Learning Grounds page, you can download excellent resources for transforming school grounds. We particularly like these books, which you can purchase or download free from the site: *Design Ideas for the Outdoor Classroom: Dig it, Plant it, Build it, Paint it!* and *All Hands in the Dirt: A Guide to Designing and Creating Natural School Grounds.* (See descriptions on pages 53 to 54.)

The Garden Classroom
www.lifelab.org/classroom.php

Photographs and a downloadable map reveal the exciting variety of features at this model school garden learning center located at the LifeLab Science Program headquarters on the grounds of the University of California at Santa Cruz. You can download a garden scavenger hunt for students to use with the map.

Montgomery High School's Native Plant Garden
http://nativeplants-geo.org/index.html

Photographs bring to life how a field littered with trash and overgrown with weeds was transformed into a vibrant California native plant garden. An interactive map links you to images, descriptions, plant lists, and ethnobotanical information for each of the natural communities represented in the garden. You can also see samples of student work and learn how the garden has become a vital part of the school's curriculum.

National Wildlife Federation Schoolyard Habitats
www.nwf.org/schoolyardhabitats

The National Wildlife Federation has some of the best resources we've found for designing and implementing wildlife-friendly outdoor classrooms. The site features resources and a description of how schools can become certified as NWF Schoolyard Habitat sites. You can also call (800) 822-9919 for information.

Roots and Shoots School Garden
http://organizations.rockbridge.net/rootsnshoots/menu.html

In the Harrington Waddell Elementary School garden, young students (shoots) work alongside older community members (roots). Web visitors can view a map of the garden and take a virtual tour of individual theme gardens. You can also order the project's *Down to Earth Handbook*, a step-by-step guide to implementing an intergenerational garden, or rent a slide show to use when presenting your garden project idea to community members or school administrators.

School Grounds Transformation
www.schoolgrounds.ca/home.html

Since 1996, the Canadian Biodiversity Institute has helped transform school-yards. This site provides support for tackling such a project, from plant selection to site design. It's furnished with images, project descriptions, and plant lists, and includes a section visitors can use to showcase schoolyard projects.

Web Resources for School Grounds
www.greenteacher.org

Compiled by *Green Teacher* magazine and Green Brick Road, this searchable database of environmental education resources provides access to books, articles, Web sites, and information on programs and organizations.

Listservs

School Gardening Listserv

This free Listserv provides a forum for educators to exchange ideas, challenges, and successes related to school gardens. To subscribe, send a message to *majordomo@ag.arizona.edu*. In the body of the message, type: subscribe school_garden digest

Schoolyard Habitat Listserv

This free Listserv, managed by the National Wildlife Federation, provides a forum for educators to exchange ideas, challenges, and successes on outdoor classroom design, curriculum integration, and more. To subscribe, send a blank e-mail to *syh-exchange-subscribe@igc.topica.com*

Books

All Hands in the Dirt: A Guide to Designing and Creating Natural School Grounds. Randee Holmes and Cam Collyer. 2000. Evergreen, Toronto, Canada. This manual will guide you through the planning process, providing tips and templates for designing a site that reflects your local natural environment and the ideas of all involved. (You can download a copy from the Evergreen Web site listed on previous page.)

Children's Gardens: A Field Guide for Teachers, Parents, and Volunteers. Elizabeth Bremner and John Pusey. 1999. University of California Cooperative Extension, Oakland, CA. Rife with advice on planning, planting, and sustaining a children's garden, this book is a great resource for a burgeoning schoolyard project. Includes a guide to resources and an annotated bibliography. Available from the Common Ground Garden Program at the University of California Cooperative Extension: (323) 838-4540.

Design Ideas for the Outdoor Classroom: Dig it, Plant it, Build it, Paint it! Evergreen Foundation. 1996. Evergreen, Toronto, Canada. This 100-page easy-to-follow guide has collections of ideas and techniques for creating native plant and vegetable gardens and a whole range of built and artistic schoolyard features. It also includes a host of resources. (You can download a copy from the Evergreen Web site listed on page 52.)

Down to Earth Handbook. Dirck and Molly Brown. 1999. Sideline Designs, Lexington, VA. This 200-page handbook created by Harrington Waddell Elementary Roots and Shoots school garden coordinators offers guidance for implementing a school garden program. It features advice on creating theme gardens, lesson plans, and tips on garnering support. You can order the handbook and a video about the project from the Roots and Shoots Web site: *http://organizations.rockbridge.net/rootsnshoots/menu.html*

The Edible Schoolyard. Margo Crabtree, ed. 1999. Learning in the Real World, Berkeley, CA. The Edible Schoolyard portrays the challenges and triumphs associated with creating a model garden project at the Martin Luther King Jr. Middle School in Berkeley, CA. Authors include project founder Alice Waters and Edible Schoolyard staff and faculty. Available from the Center for Ecoliteracy: *www.ecoliteracy.org/*

Getting Started: A Guide for Creating School Gardens as Outdoor Classrooms. Center for Ecoliteracy and Life Lab Science Program. 1997. California Department of Education, Sacramento, CA. This step-by-step guide suggests how to create a garden to use as a context for learning across the curriculum. Available from the Center for Ecoliteracy: *www.ecoliteracy.org/*

Greening School Grounds: Creating Habitats for Learning. Tim Grant and Gail Littlejohn, eds. 2001. New Society Publishers, British Colombia, Canada. This anthology features descriptions of more than a dozen schoolyard habitat and garden projects, from rooftop gardens to prairie restorations, and offers advice on bringing them to life. Includes practical tips, activities, curriculum links, and a bibliography.

Landscapes for Learning: Creating Outdoor Environments for Children and Youth. Sharon Stine. 1996. John Wiley & Sons, Somerset, NJ. Written from the perspective of a landscape architect, the book uses case studies to describe the design concepts and processes associated with creating outdoor learning environments. The author examines how the interaction between designers, teachers, and children affects the planning, building, and use of an outdoor space.

Nourishing Choices: Implementing Food Education in Classrooms, Cafeterias, and Schoolyards. Eve Pranis. 2008. National Gardening Association, South Burlington, VT. Drawing on a wealth of collective experience, *Nourishing Choices* offers a roadmap for developing a food education program and exciting children about healthful eating. It features details on ensuring sustainability and profiles of winning school- and district-based initiatives. Available from NGA's Gardening with Kids catalog (*www.gardeningwithkids.org*) or by calling (800) 538-7476.

Schoolyard Ecology Leaders' Handbook. (Online publication.) Institute of Ecosystem Studies. 2000. Millbrook, NY. This Web-based publication was written by leaders of an exemplary teacher enhancement project, Schoolyard Ecology for Elementary School Teachers. It is intended for those who support teachers in their use of school grounds for inquiry-based teaching of ecology. The publication is a work in progress featuring suggestions for effective professional development workshops and systems, curriculum frameworks, and comprehensive annotated resources.

Steps to a Bountiful Kids' Garden. Amy Gifford, ed. 2001. National Gardening Association, South Burlington, VT. Created by an organization that has gardened with kids for more than 20 years, the book advises readers on initiating and sustaining a school garden project, from getting administrative support and funds through picking and using the harvest. Available from NGA's Gardening with Kids catalog (*www.gardeningwithkids.org*) or by calling (800) 538-7476.

Journals and Articles

Transforming School Grounds. *Green Teacher* magazine. This issue of *Green Teacher* features 13 articles on topics such as schoolyard tree nurseries, butterfly gardens, and other environmental projects and curriculum connections. To request a copy of "Transforming School Grounds" (issue #47), contact *Green Teacher*, P.O. Box 452, Niagara Falls, NY 14304; (888) 804-1486.

The following articles, which are related to the material in this book, can be found on the National Gardening Association's Web sites, *www.garden.org* and *www.kidsgardening.org*. You can search the extensive article databases on each of these sister sites for further inspiration and advice.

Landscaping for the Birds
www.garden.org/articles/articles.php?q=show&id=190

Make Your Own Weather Station
www.fi.edu/weather/todo/todo.html

Organic Matters (Building Healthy Soil)
www.garden.org/articles/articles.php?q=show&id=101

Planning Learning Landscapes: Students Lead the Way
www.kidsgardening.org/Dig/DigDetail.taf?ID=1719&Type=Art

The Rotten Truth: Cultivating Compost
www.kidsgardening.org/Dig/DigDetail.taf?ID=1152&Type=Art

The Secret Life of Ponds
www.kidsgardening.org/Dig/DigDetail.taf?ID=1715&Type=Art

Would-Be Wood (recycled plastic lumber)
www.garden.org/articles/articles.php?q=show&id=1130

Videos

A Crack in the Pavement. In this energetic two-part series, Canadian youngsters, teachers, and community members share feelings and advice about working together to turn schoolyards into thriving green oases. Available from Bullfrog films. Phone: (800) 543-FROG; Web site: *www.bullfrogfilms.com/catalog/crack.html*

The Schoolyard Habitats® Program. This video showcases more than 25 National Wildlife Federation Schoolyard Habitat sites across the United States. Students, educators, administrators, parents, and community members describe the benefits of creating a wildlife habitat in the educational setting. An excellent tool for those who need to justify an outdoor classroom to school administrators. Available through the National Wildlife Federation: *www.nwf.org*

Supplies

Gardening with Kids Catalog. The National Gardening Association's print and online catalog of garden-based educational tools and curricula, and products for outdoor and indoor gardening. Contact National Gardening Association, 1100 Dorset Street, South Burlington, VT 05403; (800) 538-7476; or visit *www.gardeningwithkids.org*

Gardening with Kids Resource Catalog

School and youth gardens are ideal vehicles for teaching across the curriculum, enlivening learning, and helping young people develop lifelong social skills. The *Gardening with Kids* resource catalog features a renowned selection of curriculum resources and equipment for indoor and outdoor gardening, as well as kid-friendly tools, raised beds and containers, worm composting and composting supplies, exclusive hands-on activity kits, and much more. Visit *www.GardeningWithKids.org*.

KidsGardening.org

Our award-winning Web site is an interactive hub where teachers, parents, and others who garden with kids find inspiration, advice, and opportunities for growth. Featuring an extensive library of lesson plans and hands-on activities, you'll also find online horticultural courses, a national School Garden Registry to find colleagues in your area willing to exchange ideas and to help problem-solve, and a regularly updated list of grants and funding sources.

Grants and Awards

NGA is proud to offer many grants throughout the school year that award cash and gardening supplies to schools and community organizations that actively engage youth in the garden. We're always expanding grant availability thanks to the generosity of our corporate sponsors, so be sure and check out the latest and greatest opportunities at *www.KidsGardening.Org/grants*.

Kids Garden News

Subscribe to this popular monthly e-mail and you'll be kept up to date on the latest grant applications and deadlines, and enjoy standards-based lessons using indoor and outdoor gardens as well as information and links to educational resources. Visit *www.KidsGardening.org* to sign up!

For more information about our programs, visit:

www.KidsGardening.org, www.GardeningWithKids.org.

The mission of the National Gardening Association is to promote home, school, and community gardening as a means to renew and sustain the essential connection between people, plants, and the environment.